# *It's Okay…*

# *Scream in the Shower!*

*An atlas of guideposts for your Grief Journey:*

*What you need to know and do when your partner passes before you.*

*Holly Chorba, RiverFlowChronicles*

Cover Design and Photographs by the author.

Copyright © 2021 by Holly Chorba

All rights reserved.
This book or any portion thereof may not be reproduced or used in any manner whatsoever without the express written permission of the publisher except for the use of brief quotations in a book review.

ISBN: 979-8-9855013-0-8
Printed by DiggyPOD, Inc., in the United States of America.
Fourth Printing, 2023
chorbasriverflowchronicles.com/
Holly Chorba
816 Buckton Road Winthrop, NY 13697
holly@chorbasriverflowchronicles.com

*TO FRIENDS WHO CARE AND THOSE WHO NEED THEM*

*When we honestly ask ourselves which people in our lives
mean the most to us,
we often find it is those who
instead of giving much advice, solutions, cures,
have chosen rather to share our pain and touch our wounds
with a gentle hand.*

*The friend who can be silent with us in a moment of despair or confusion,
who can stay with us in an hour of grief and bereavement,
who can tolerate not knowing, not curing, not healing
and face with us the reality of our own powerlessness,
that is the friend who cares.*
*(Henri Nouwen)*

## CONTENTS

Preface…iii

CRUCIAL PRACTICES:…vi

Acknowledgements…xi

Introduction: Come, get a hug…xiii

Phases I, II, III…1

End Note…104

Appendix…105

# CONTENTS (Phases I, II, and III)

## PHASE I, IMMEDIATE SURVIVAL …1

    Guidepost I-A: Physical and Emotional Being…3

    Guidepost I-B: Communicating and Relating…14

    Guidepost I-C: Spiritual Solace and Evolution…23

    PRACTICE I WITH YOUR MEDITATIVE COMPANION…31

## PHASE II, REGAINING YOUR BALANCE … 43

    Guidepost II-A: Physical and Emotional Being…44

    Guidepost II-B: Communicating and Relating…51

    Guidepost II-C: Spiritual Solace and Evolution…63

    PRACTICE II WITH YOUR MEDITATIVE COMPANION…69

## PHASE III, LIFE AFTER LOSS …79

    Guidepost III-A: Physical and Emotional Being…81

    Guidepost III-B: Communicating and Relating…86

    Guidepost III-C: Spiritual Solace and Evolution…93

    PRACTICE III WITH YOUR MEDITATIVE COMPANION…95

# *Preface*

Immediate Practical Advice. HOW DO YOU POSSIBLY EVEN START?

Read this today! The information below was written by my friend Linda Sparks and e-mailed to me at my request within days of my husband Ron's death. It was my lifeline…directing me to take immediate actions needed to deal with unexpected trauma. It has proven invaluable to me and several other recently bereaved friends since. It also served as the inspiration for me to write to you. Check it out. Check whether updates or locale specifics are needed, and get started taking care of the most pressing needs you have following the death of your most significant other. Listings of suggested practices for you to follow end the preface and are embedded throughout this book. You may want to write your responses as you read and negotiate these difficult, complicated times.

Hugs to you. I am sorry for your loss. *Holly Chorba*

## Linda's E-Mail

*"Hubby is dead. What do you do next???"*

*"Send everybody on his email address book an email notifying them. They will want to know. Many of these folks will send back fond memories of your hubby that you never knew a thing about. It will help you feel better. Send similar email to your address book. Don't delegate this to somebody else--the personal things you want to say won't get said. Call those few friends/family closest to you.*

*"Mortuary. There's only one in Green Valley, but do you really want to drive to Tucson? Take with you names of husband's parents, you'll need it for The death certificate. Funeral or cremation, you'll have to decide. If you*

*choose cremation, tell them you'll bring your own container—their cardboard box costs $70. You can put him in a shoe box or an Indian pot; you can even make your own container. They're going to give him to you in a plastic bag anyway. They tax you for cremation. Going rate for baseline cremation is currently $1500+/-. You pay them then and there, so take credit card or check book.*

*"Death certificates. Know how many you will need when you go to the mortuary. One for every bank, Mutual Fund company (IRAs or regular accounts), trust companies, SSA, each pension, each house, cars, insurance, you name it and you'll need one for it. They cost $15 each and were part of the $1500 above. However, I found that most institutions will make a copy and return the one you give them, so don't go overboard –5 or 6 will do.*

*"Homeowner's/car insurance company. Call them early on as they are very helpful. Get policies moved to your name. Keep record of person you talked to, time, date, follow-up if necessary.*

*"Trust company. They should have been at the top of your email list. If you have a good trust and a good trust officer, life will be easier—no probate.*

*"Lawyer. If you don't have a trust, you will need a lawyer (probably the one who's been updating your wills, etc. You will have to go through probate. Call him/her and set the wheels in progress.*

*"Life insurance. If your husband had it, make this call soonest and get the paperwork started. Keep record of person you talked to, time, date, follow-up necessary.*

*"Social Security, VA, pension plans. Notify of death. Keep record of person you talked to, time, date, follow-up if necessary. Some pay backward, some pay forward—this matters to you. Law requires VA to pay surviving spouse the payment for the month your husband died. SSA does not let you keep the payment for the month during which your husband died, you*

*will have to send it back—but you don't have to do so immediately. They will send you $255 death benefit, but don't hold your breath until it comes. Your husband's employment pension could do either. If you have survivor benefits coming, be sure to state that as there are forms they have to mail to you. Expect to get stupid mailings asking your husband to confirm that he's alive—obviously, he's not.*

*"IRA's. Call each Fund company. They have separate departments for surviving beneficiaries and they are helpful and compassionate. Keep record of person you talked to, time, date, follow-up necessary. You will have several choices as the sole primary beneficiary (spouse) of an IRA, i.e. "keep as own," "cash out," etc. What you do will depend on your age and financial circumstance and you'll have plenty of time to decide after the paperwork arrives. This call is just getting them to send you the paperwork.*

*"Bank accounts. Don't take hubby's name off your bank account for at least 6 months following his death (at which time, you'll need a death certificate.) If a check comes in, you'll have a devil of a time cashing it if his name isn't on an account. Talk to your trust officer about whether you should change your bank account to "payable on death: or "transfer on death" to your trust.*

*"Cars. Until it's paid off you don't have a title. Without the title, taking his name off the car requires letters to and from the lender. Why bother? He's not going to be driving it, so his name on the title is of no consequence. After it's paid off, talk to trust officer or lawyer to decide how to title it.*

*"Utilities. At some point you'll have to get these in your name only. There are varying degrees of hassle depending on the company. So don't bother until you're up to the hassle. Some will require credit checks, so do them after all your finances are settled down. Some will require that they talk to the dead account holder—no kidding—before removing his name. Bear up.*

"Return anything you personally don't need (hearing aid batteries, incontinent supplies, denture cleaner, etc) that was recently purchased and not used, to the point of purchase. Walgreen's doesn't make it easy, Walmart is gracious and a breeze. Cancel any classes/trips hubby was scheduled to take before the start date. It's money in your pocket. After the start date, it's money you'll never see again.

"Decide what you want to do with his clothes, shoes, personal items, books, etc. Family and close friends may want mementos (some even want copies of the death certificates). Get with it and move that stuff on to wherever you choose, but move it. Some people leave it all untouched for years—he's not coming back for it. And sometimes, you feel as if it's criminal to move it out, because he'll need it. He won't! But there are a lot of folks in this world who need a pair of pants or shoes, so help them and yourself—move it out.

"See friends, take classes, keep up with your activities. You have a lot of life left in you and hubby would want you to live it. Go out for lunch and dinner. Talk about your husband; your friends loved him too and want to reminisce about the good times. Cry when you have to, but don't get lost in it. Say good night to him every night.

"Don't be surprised if you can't stand to cook for one, don't want to eat and, lose weight. The day may come when anything not moving looks good to eat and you gain all the weight back. Don't be surprised if it's almost impossible to do alone the things you used to do with him. Find a hobby you didn't share with him.

"Expect it to take a long time for complete recovery. You'll think you're fine and then months later fall into a well of despair. Climb out. Get moving, do something. Don't expect to tick off the 7 stages of grief—you may miss quite a few of them and find your very own stage or two."

*Linda Sparks, (2009)*

At a loss on where to begin? Practices based on Linda's advice are listed beginning on the next page.

Determine whether updates or locale specifics are needed, and get started taking care of the most pressing needs you have following the death of your most significant other. You most likely have already notified those you love of your significant other's passing. Perhaps you've relied on close family or friends to help you. It is a difficult task; be bolstered if it has been accomplished. Decide and act. You may choose to copy the upper case, bold, bulleted lists into a notebook or journal or add your responses herein as you log your own Grief Journey.

Crucial Practices in this section can be invaluable as well if addressed BEFORE that death of a significant other and even before your own death to help your loved ones who will grieve you. Begin today!

The Guideposts that follow the Introduction can help you, or someone you care for, deal with many kinds of losses: death, divorce, injury, health, a loved home, a treasured ability.

# *Crucial Practices to meet your immediate needs:*

*I CAN RELY ON THE FOLLOWING PEOPLE FOR HELP REGARDING:*

- 

- 

*I WILL NOTIFY LOVED ONES AS FOLLOWS:*

- 

- 

*I WILL NOTIFY IMPORTANT ASSOCIATES AS FOLLOWS:*

- 

- 

*I NOTIFY THOSE WHOSE IMPORTANCE TO THE DECEASED IS UNKNOWN BY:*

-

*MY UP-TO-DATE EMERGENCY CONTACT IS:*

- 

- 

*MY CONFIDANT NOTIFIED OF LOCATIONS OF MY IMPORTANT INFORMATION :*

- 

- 

## RECORD of my DOCUMENT LOCATION:

- **BIRTH CERTIFICATE**

- 

- **SOCIAL SECURITY CARD**

- **INSURANCE PAPERS**

-

- RETIREMENT ACCOUNTS, ANNUITIES
- INVESTMENTS, STOCK CERTIFICATES
- WILLS AND TRUSTS
- LIVING WILL
- DO NOT RESUSCITATE ORDERS
- PRE-BURIAL ARRANGEMENTS
- PHYSICIAN NAME
- DENTIST NAME
- LAWYER NAME
- POWERS OF ATTORNEY
- BANK STATEMENTS
- TITLES
- DEEDS
- SAFETY DEPOSIT BOXES
- SAFETY DEPOSIT KEYS
- OTHER KEYS
- PASSWORDS
- ADDRESS BOOK
- DEATH CERTIFICATES

# RECORD of DATES: EARLY NOTIFICATION TO :

- **LIFE INSURANCE COMPANY**

- **HOMEOWNER AND CAR INSURANCE COMPANIES**

- **LAWYER**

- **SOCIAL SECURITY OFFICE**

- **PENSION /RETIREMENT COMPANIES**

- **RETIREMENT ACCOUNT**

- **FUNERAL HOME, CREMATORY OR OTHER**

## *RECORD of DATES / LATER NOTIFICATIONS :*

## *(SEEK PROFESSIONAL ADVICE ON HOW AND WHEN TO MAKE ANY CHANGES)*

- *BANK ACCOUNTS*

- *CAR TITLES*

- *UTILITY COMPANIES*

- *ITEMS TO BE RETURNED*

- *APPOINTMENTS TO BE CANCELLED*

- *MEMENTOS TO BE DISTRIBUTED*

Periodically come back to these lists, check your progress and modify them as your journey continues. Continue reading when you feel ready. That may be in days, weeks, or months.

Check the practices whenever you feel the need for someone to reach out to you in empathy. Then, as you have had some time to contemplate your being as a recently bereaved grieving person, read on!

You are not alone. I am here for you through this book. You will read of many others who are here for you too. They and you have suffered heart-wrenching loss. Your world has inexorably changed.

Each of you has lost a different beloved person. Each of you had a different relationship, different experiences, different plans. Your loss may have occurred suddenly due to accident or intent, expectedly after illness or injury, or because of advanced or premature age. You may or may not have been with your loved one when he died. Each of you now has access to different resources for your remaining years, including physical, emotional, and spiritual ones. Yet all of us have much to share.

This book offers comfort, support and direction. Of course I am not you; I am just another one who has suffered such loss. Now, after several years, I live with grace and peace of mind. That is what I want for you. I want you to survive and develop a new perspective on life that promotes the serenity you seek.

Life for me turned upside down and backwards. I was distraught; I needed support to function on a daily basis. Others were there for me; they provided the support, reassurance, and comfort I needed. This book offers you sympathy, empathy, virtual hugs, shared experiences and survival strategies.

The guideposts of the book are organized into three parts that lead from overwhelming grief to graceful life: Phase I, Immediate Survival; Phase II, Regaining Your Balance; Phase III, Life after Loss. The parts follow what was generally (for me) the early, middle and later phases of grief during the four years following the death of Ron, my husband of over 30 years.

Guideposts are offered within each Phase regarding Physical and Emotional Being, Communicating and Relating, and Spiritual Solace. These can be meaningfully read in sequence or selected in any order to illuminate whatever current issues may darken your life.

The Guideposts of each section relate to what some of my bereft friends and I have experienced. They are an offering of thoughts and actions to experiment with as you travel your own journey from rejecting loss to knowing and accepting grief, to embracing life beyond. The guideposts are there for you; you are not alone in your grief journey. What my friends and I have experienced may be different from what you are experiencing, but our experiences are something you may relate to and gain comfort from. We have traveled grief and remain on this earth better, more empathetic people than we previously were.

Each guidepost contains "Practices". These are suggested actions for you to aid your physical and emotional well-being, your communicating and relating, and your spiritual well-being. You are invited to record your responses and negotiate the challenges of your own Grief Journey.

The appendix is a list of resources that I found helpful in my journey, including in the writing of this book. I found them of use in the order in which they are listed.

# Hugs and Safe Travels, *Holly Chorba*

# *Acknowledgements*

My heartfelt thanks to the many family members and friends who have held me close along my journey. Upon Ron's death, I was in shock. I was sustained by first responders and dear friends who lived nearby, who came to me and stayed with me for days. They were evidence that I was not alone, that I had love and support. They encouraged me to do all those necessary tasks for life: eat, sleep, breath, move. Invite that for yourself, whether you are at home, in a hospice facility, hospital, nursing home or other location. You may not need that degree of support, or may need much more. A friend who lost his mother, wife and children in a horrific accident was blessed with other family members who lived with him a year. A girlfriend had her out-of-state children stay with her for a week. A widower had neighbors call daily. Welcome those who will fulfill your needs. We are forever grateful to those angels. Appreciate your angels and know how blessed you are.

"Angels" also arrived as days passed and family members and friends recognized the importance of their presence at my time of bereavement. You may be blessed by having a sibling, parent, other family member or friend who can suspend his or her normal life to be with you. Graciously accept that love.

Spiritual support is also essential at a time of loss. Find yours. Turn to what you love and need…be it family, church, the souls of deceased, nature, input from a minister or counselor, the internet, or written word and your god to provide essential healing support.

I am forever grateful to those who served as angels, giving me the love and support I needed to carry grief. A few of those had passed from this world, but their spirits were and are still alive in me, encouraging me to hold tight to life. Thank you to Ron, Mary P., Dad, Janet, and Gramma Kromer. Also to my mother, whose spirit remained strong throughout her trials. She was an inspiration to live for today despite the loss of her husband of 73 years.

Other souls were by my side. Thank you to Carol R., Jim M., Ellen, Diana, Phil and Sue, Sue K., Gail, Joyce and Kevin, Fran, Alex and Tracy, Zeke, Skyler, Francoise, Marcy and Jerry, Paul, Mike and my camera club friends, neighbors, and my book club members who were there for me in Arizona to help me deal with immediate needs. JoAnne and Jack, Ann M., Cliff, Angie, Ann and Scott, Becky, Nicole and Liz, Bob and Adeana offered essential company and encouragement as time went on.

Life-long friends and family from the East came to recognize my loss, honor Ron and my relationship with him, and help me find my balance. I am indebted to Frank and Maureen, Dean and Nona, Jeffrey, Carol J., Donna, my New York book club, Penny and Bob and family, Keri, Ann J., Carolyn and Gene, Sonmez and Jane, Bill, Pam and Ben, Fernando, Sally and Lariah, Mary, Margarette and Boyd, Ashley, Paul, Donna and Mike, Valerie…thank you all!

Several friends gave wonderful support via mail, e-mails or phone calls. Kalpana, Robin, Rich G., Jim S., David and Kathy, and Marilyn and Glenn, thank you for your kind words. Robin provided invaluable counseling in-person and via e-mail.

The writing of this work was greatly helped by countless discussions regarding managing grief with Ellen, Kathy, Penny, Sally, Dr. A. Bhagat, and Ashley. They each helped me translate my emotions and experiences regarding grief into the words I pass along to you.

Linda Sparks wrote the preface, prior to my writing this. It has been of value to many bereft friends. Valerie Dunning, my editor during our years in education, again put her knowledge and talents toward making this work clear and correct. Jeanne Rouselle provided expert advice on how to present my ideas in a user-friendly format and get it into the hands of a printer. Ashley and Beth read final copy, providing a fresh perspective and large view of the work.

# Introduction

*Come get a hug!*

You have lost the person most important to you in life. You are likely overcome with negative emotions. You may even feel that no-one has ever been this distraught, or that no-one has ever survived such a loss. The idea of throwing yourself onto the funeral pyre and ending your grief may be quite attractive. You may want to join your significant other in heaven. You may feel that there is nothing left for you on this earth, that your very reason for being is gone.

Wait! Be patient with yourself! You are not alone. Others have survived and learned to carry such grief. They have found a different course in their lives such that they do have reason to continue. This earth holds many joys for you yet. Those others are available to help you. Love is here on this earth for you. The guideposts in this book mark the way several close friends and I have survived such a loss and lived. Read on! Hang on!

You are one of the reasons that I am still here, to share how I've survived the loss of my husband of thirty years. The experience was a shock to me. My husband Ron had endured many years of heart disease and related health problems, including five stays in the critical care unit of 3 different hospitals, yet his death was an unexpected trauma for me. He was 76 years old and had told me that he would "never make 80." Yet for months after he passed, I could not even speak the words "my husband died." I had not internalized death as the inevitability it is, for him, for me, for us all. Since then I have recognized that, as little as we like it, the death of a spouse will be suffered by millions in the United States each year.

When my life exploded, I tried to put it back together again as it had been. I could not. The biggest piece was missing. At first, the very idea of survival or potential growth appalled me. I felt it meant letting go of much of what I once had, letting go of the physical presence of Ron. Only after time did I realize that letting go was a necessary gateway to proceeding in life and that I had to forge a different whole.

You do not have to let go yet. You can determine to survive, grow, adapt and change gradually…according to your own time frame. Be patient and gentle with yourself. Be comforted in the realization that you are not alone in your grief, not alone no matter how distraught you are feeling. Someone, somewhere, has felt similarly and survived. You too are surviving if you are reading this book.

Seek refuge in your faith, family, and friends. These guideposts mark a path to feeling their love as you negotiate your distraught present.

# *PHASE I*

# *IMMEDIATE SURVIVAL*

*Nothing Gold Can Stay*

*Nature's first green is gold,*

*Her hardest hue to hold.*

*Her early leaf's a flower;*

*But only so an hour.*

*Then leaf subsides to leaf.*

*(Robert Frost)*

NATURE'S FIRST GREEN

HOSPICE OFFICE SIGN

# Guidepost I-A: Physical and Emotional Being

You are reading "IT"S OKAY…SCREAM IN THE SHOWER!" In fact it is advisable to scream in the shower! It's a way to reclaim yourself. GRIEVE! Grief is all that makes sense right now.

Own your emotions. Allow yourself time to feel the blow you've been dealt and to eventually heal. Turn inward and spend time meeting your needs, be they to sleep more, pray, meditate, scream, block out everyone, be alone, be constantly with another, stop eating or binge eat. Just do no harm to yourself or others.

The most important thing you lose when your most significant other dies is LOVE. Those of you who were lucky shared love until death did the parting. Love is what life is all about. Accept that you are injured, despairing, distraught. Until you feel better recognize that you need time to heal. Seek whatever comforts you; indulge in it. Some people withdraw, stay in bed for days, in the house for weeks. Some cannot be alone and surround themselves with activity. Some seek silence, church, counseling, or family, friends or even strangers.

Feel what you feel, recognize it, but also recognize that whatever it is that you feel, you won't feel this way forever. Emotions are temporary. You may grieve forever, miss your significant-other forever, wish he or she were with you here forever. Regardless, you won't hurt like this forever. Life will not allow that. You, as you continue to live, will learn to feel life again. It was easy for me to bury myself in quiet desperation, not doing anything but sitting around thinking about whom and what I'd lost. I could not focus on any entertainment; it seemed totally incongruous. I could read book after book about grief and loss, and was somewhat comforted in the knowledge that the authors had apparently survived, at least long enough to tell their tales. It helped too that the end of every story was a different life, not better or worse, not replacing what had been, simply different with its own concerns, satisfactions, and joys. These longer books were my internal mental life for months. Gradually, I seemed to have gained all I could from them: a sense that I was not alone in grief, that the human condition involved such times for just about everyone, that no-one gets out of life alive. We each will lose or be lost. Since my husband had frequently said that he could not live without me I began to feel that I owed it to him to try to keep living.

You probably will realize that people remain on this earth whom you love: family, friends, humanity. Accept that love in your life. When you can summon up the energy, spend time with those people and grieve with those who are also grieving your loss.

When your significant other has died, you will hear "I'm sorry." Chances are, you will hear these words frequently. Most of the time they will actually help, at least a little bit, at least more than when they are not offered. But, let's get right to some other words that you need to hear.

"IT IS OKAY…SCREAM IN THE SHOWER!" Actually, it's more than okay. It can do you a lot of good to express the grief you feel, be it anger, despondency, relief, gratitude, sorrow, isolation, or fear. Screams can release emotion, so can howling at the moon, or shaking out yourself physically. Try out these releases; see if any work for you.

You may be swamped by so much emotion that you'll feel your leg has just been cut off at the waist. My friend's husband passed on. She felt she'd been "ripped in half." Life felt torn asunder. Expectations, from those of tomorrow until you no longer exist, are dashed. It can be overwhelming.

Therefore, it's okay to scream in the shower, or in the car, or the closet, or wherever else you can find that the troops won't come running when they hear you. And when you do scream, you may find as I did, for whatever reason if only to shed some emotionality, it helps. So go ahead...find your spot...try it. Nothing lost if it doesn't help. At least you'll know that someone else felt such despair, such outrage, such pain that she screamed in the shower...and lived to recommend it.

Keep in mind that I do not purport to be an expert on grief. Mine is just one take, and I've read and experienced that there are no experts; that each grief stricken person has faced a different loss, a unique relationship that is now missing and has encountered different life and death circumstances.

Whatever your past experiences, your loss will shape your realization and eventual acceptance regarding the mortality of your loved one and of yourself. Of course, it will also shape how you deal with loss itself. Initially you may not be afraid of death anymore; in fact in wanting your grief to end, you may even come to welcome death! If so, it is important that you realize that life is precious and fleeting, a gift that is the PRESENT. The realization of the temporary nature of life is a good thing. Grasp on to whatever beauty you see in life, be it natural or man-made creations, travel, work, volunteerism, creative expression, physical maintenance, caring for family, friends, or strangers. Appreciate the love and abilities as well as the material blessings that you have. Count your blessings nightly!

You have lived thus far with love that still exists; find it, take refuge in it! Regardless of the different experiences and the different types of significant relationships, recognize that millions of others have experienced a loss of their life partner and yet continue on a life's path, albeit altered from their previous expectations.

Experiences that you have had in losing others who had been close to you can especially affect you. I had been extremely blessed. Until I was 62 years old, I had lost only my elderly grandparents and distant friends. Then six years before my husband died, I lost a very close friend and much of her young family in a car accident, followed by the loss of other friends. Two years before Ron's passing, I lost my father. Concurrently, there were concerns with my mother's and sister's health. I felt terribly threatened with loss; then my husband passed away. At that point I became overwhelmed.

I learned that accepting grief, allowing myself to grieve by screaming in the shower (Pick your own manner of release.) was essential for moving beyond immobilizing grief. I've learned that EMOTIONS ARE TEMPORARY. No matter how intense, how seemingly long-lived, emotions do change. No matter how low you feel on one day, another day you won't feel quite as bad. WAIT becomes a good mantra, one that can see you through to something better. Life won't ever be the same, true enough. You may always miss your husband and wish he were physically with you. You may always wish that it was you who had passed first.

You may read what I have to say and disagree. Take my statement that "Emotions are temporary." My friend who lost her husband six months after I lost mine found that emotions are more aptly "forever changing". One day she felt like she had made some progress, and then the next day or week, she was back to square one. She felt that her emotions had progressed very little and that she could easily slip backwards and often did. It was, for her, rather like a bad storm, with waves crashing on her until she was near drowning, emotions often reverting to their original state. Yet they do eventually change. The frequency and intensity of the most destructive emotions lessen, and gradually positive emotions make their way into the psyche.

Take the time to pamper yourself with comfort food, massages, touch physical therapy, spending time with friends and family, hugging, talking, and just being present. You have suffered a grave injury; treat yourself gently to promote healing.

Express yourself physically in ways other than screaming. Dress to fit how you feel. Traditionally that is wearing black; black may or may not fit your needs. You may also want to dress surrounded by your loved one, wrapped in her sweater or sleeping in his tee shirt. You may choose dowdy clothes, or clothes that reflect your desire to be part of your circle. Do what is comfortable for you. Wearing jewelry is another way to experience and express your loss and be comfortable in how you are feeling. Choices, fitting to some people and not others, include: make no change, wear no or minimal jewelry, wear jewelry of the deceased; wear your wedding ring as usual or in a different way (perhaps on a necklace, or on the right hand); wear special jewelry such as a locket with your loved one's photo or a bracelet containing his or her ashes. These non-verbal ways of expressing yourself help you and others to be together, to understand each other.

Travel was a physical and emotional experience for me in the early phase of grief. Ron died at home, and at first I could not venture out the front door, could not get in a car, could not "travel" beyond my rooms. I needed to process that he would not be coming home, that he no longer could accept my help to care for him…that he was not on this earth for me. It was not until his ashes arrived from the crematory that I felt okay leaving the house. It took my sister or grandson accompanying me for moral support to go to the funeral home, doctor's office and bank. Weeks later I found I could walk in the neighborhood, and when accompanied by a friend, visit old haunts to say goodbye. Months later, I found my saviors, friends who offered to drive me across the country to my summer home. A month after that, I could take an airplane trip only because my brother agreed to accompany me on a visit to our mom. (She was suffering from dementia and unaware of Ron's passing.)

Doctors and other physical caregivers may be a service that you gravitate to or shun. I found myself keeping appointments, though set back when asked for an emergency contact number. Be prepared! Your "normal" emergency contact is no longer available! Touch physical therapy was a therapy I had already been using and found extremely healing after my loss. Diet supplements I did not care to take; even prescriptions were put off for a while (not a good idea!).

I vacillated between wanting to maintain health and not caring to deal with myself. Urge yourself to maintain healthy habits.

Recognize too that as little as we like it, experiencing the death of our most significant other will happen to millions of us in the United States each year. This is a miserable, but true, little fact. It's possible that you can't believe this, especially that your spouse has passed before you have. I had trouble with this one myself. Even now it sometimes seems that Ron will be back, that his absence is a bad dream, that HE SHOULD BE HERE! Well, he should be! I want him back; he would still enjoy it here. We could do all those cool things we'd planned. Time seems to be the sole factor that is bringing me to realize that he won't be coming back. I want my Catholic upbringing to be accurate...that at least we'll meet in heaven someday. On this earth, I can only evoke his spirit; be thankful for what we shared and continue sharing the parts of me that were "us".

Gradually, this focus on only the loss subsides. One day you will find that instead of wondering how the birds can possibly still sing, or how the sun can come up each morning, you are appreciating the simple joy of a child's laughter or enjoying the beauty of the forest or park. At first you will find that there is at least something to feel neutral or numb about, and then find there is something that actually brings a smile. Be patient, you will stop feeling guilty that you are still here to enjoy life. Joy still exists for you. Allow yourself that.

## *Practices to Aid Physical and Emotional Being:*

*THE ULTIMATE GOAL: TO BE AT PEACE WITH YOUR LIFE AS YOU KNOW IT... TODAY. (LIZ DIVIO, 2013)*
*AND TO REJOICE IN YOUR LIFE AS YOU KNOW IT...TODAY. (HOLLY CHORBA)*

Realize that you are entering a new phase of life, one without the significant other whom you have recently lost. You have a variety of needs to honor and memorialize your loved one and to find your bearings in a life without him or her. Take your time; your emotions, senses, and thoughts, even your body, are in flux. Be patient and gentle with yourself as you experience this time in your life.

Learn behaviors that will promote the healing of the terrible wound associated with grief. You lost a large part of yourself when you lost your loved one. Much like suffering an amputated limb, you are bound to feel pain, phantom pain. Time and attention are needed to heal. You will likely carry the grief you feel forever, yet the pain from the wound will lessen, perhaps even cease.

What you seek for input to your thoughts and emotions, what you promote for output of your voice and writing, and what behaviors you allow and insist on can move you toward a re-developed life.

Recognize now how you are feeling; it is your time to grieve. Be gentle with yourself. Communicate with yourself here, in your Grief Journal notebook, or with a friend, family member or a counselor. Designate a private, limited time each day to absorb your loss, and memorialize your loved one in your thoughts. Some like to do this just before bedtime through prayer, by saying, "Goodnight and Thank you," to their dearly departed, or when lighting a candle upon awakening, by viewing photographs of the loved one, by re-

reading sympathy cards, eulogies, or letters and e-mails, or by thinking loving thoughts directed to the spirit of the loved one at sunrise.

Below are suggestions for entries into your journal.

***MY MEANS OF HONORING MY LOVED ONE EACH DAY WILL BE TO :***

- 
- 
- 

***TIME OF DAY AND DURATION OF THIS DEVOTION:***

- 

Chances are you have physical symptoms of your grief. Write them in your journal, and decide if you need help dealing with them. Examples of symptoms are: sleeplessness, digestive upset, racing heart, tenseness, frequent crying spells, withdrawal, depression, frantic activity, confusion, or difficulty focusing. Examples of ways to heal include: walking (nature-walks worked for me!), talking to friends, family, clergy or counselor(s), attending church, listening to music, medications, making lists of what to do, or setting about attending to items in the Preface. (Check your progress on the lists that you have drawn up.) Avoid unhealthy coping mechanisms.

**MY PHYSICAL SYMPTOMS/ MY PRESCRIPTIONS TO HEAL**

-

Recognize too that emotions are temporary, and how you feel now is appropriate, yet not how you will feel in a year. Select a book, television program, or other media and access regular positive input to draw you back to the world of the living. What you fill your head with is particularly important after such a loss. Your individual likes and dislikes will determine what you are open to. Whichever it is, it is likely you'll be able to focus only for a short time. It's essential that you select some form of positive input to draw you back into the world of the living. Reading appeals to some. There are several books of short passages supplying a few paragraphs or less a day that can direct your mind in positive ways.(See Appendix.) Here is one of my favorite short readings that I read frequently:

*Look To this Day*

*Look to this day*

*For it is the very Life of Life.*

*In its brief course lie all the verities and realities of your existence:*

*The Glory of Action,*

*The Bliss of Growth,*

*The Splendor of Beauty.*

*For Yesterday is but a dream and tomorrow is only a vision.*

*But today well-lived makes every yesterday a dream of happiness and every*

*tomorrow a vision of hope.*

*Look well, therefore, to THIS DAY. (Anonymous)*

This really helped, and still helps me, to keep my head on straight! It also helped me to jot down short reminders to be positive, which were gleaned for my readings, and to post them on the mirror to view each morning. Early on mine were: 'Maintain Focus,...Remain Here... Be Positive... Thank God for nature, comfort, and finding heaven on earth...and ...I am Loved."

*POSITIVE INPUT EACH DAY WILL COME FROM :*

- 
- 

*REMINDERS I WILL POST ARE:*

- 
- 

*I AM ON THIS EARTH BECAUSE:*

- 
- 

*MY PURPOSES IN LIFE ARE:*

- 
-

Travel! Get out of the house, even to just breathe fresh air and stand in the backyard or a park. Get out and attend to the business at hand. Meet with the funeral director. Go to the social security and doctor's offices. Attend memorials, distribute ashes, visit the places your colleagues are. You should gradually evolve to be rejoining the community. Make it a goal to get outside each day if only to get the mail!

*I AM OUTSIDE THE HOUSE WITH OTHERS WHEN I:*

-

# Guidepost I-B: Communicating and Relating

Let's talk about SUPPORT. The support that I needed immediately was there, and I'd accepted the very excellent advice I'd been given to welcome help offered and to let family and friends know what I needed. Thinking back on that support gives me comfort still. Perhaps you have just lost a spouse who was bonded to you practically, intellectually, emotionally, and physically. It's a huge part of you that is no longer. You may be in shock and need input just to survive, to think clearly, and to behave rationally.

Communications and relationships provide healing energy through love. The most important communication is BEING THERE. The presence of those who care about you is primary. Recognize this, even if those close to you don't have the right words, even if they cannot say any words. Their time spent with you is a gift. It tells you that you are not alone, not even now when you've lost one who may well have been the most important person in your life, a person who was actually part of you. You may be lucky and have someone (or a few people) come to stay with you if you need that. The presence of others was best for me. I understood that I wasn't good company; I slept odd hours, was depressed, needed encouragement to eat, and to move, but I did appreciate the hugs, smiles, pampering, and even being left alone or "ignored" when appropriate. Perhaps it was the latter that I appreciated most. Those who absented themselves while I screamed in the shower and let that be, yet were there to be pleasant company when I could manage it, were invaluable. Recognize that those who offer to help love you. Give them the gift of acceptance; give yourself that gift too.

HUGS are an especially great gift from those close to you. Accept them. When you get a hug you give one, so take comfort and give comfort in that simple, physical, important way. HUG. The women I know who have lost a beloved husband have had a particular difficulty interpreting support, especially supportive hugs, from male friends. Emotions are running high and easily confused! A hug may feel welcome, unwelcome or even a violation. If perceived as a possible sexual come-on, it could elicit resentment and anger. There may be sexual tension in physical consolation, especially between close friends. It can be misleading to both parties. Don't be surprised if your reaction to the opposite sex is extreme. A male friend innocently hugged me with a "Hey, how are you doing," and I jumped a foot off my chair. It was simply too soon for a foreign male touch. Yet I recognized that interest from the opposite sex could be appropriate, expressing merely a friendly concern. Only you can decide what is a violation or what is welcome. You may feel it is inappropriate because the timing is wrong, or a hug may be just what you need. Each of us reacts differently, depending where we are emotionally at any given time. A recently widowed girlfriend felt the need to run home, aghast after she had summoned the courage to go out to dinner with another girlfriend, and a stranger spoke to her, showing some possible interest in connecting. An opposite reaction was felt by another friend who clung to her late husband's brother as if she were drowning; she felt saved by his support.

Your perception of others may be a bit warped by your grief. You may see their attempts to help or be comforting as interference. Self-centeredness can initially envelope one when an especially close loved one dies. I was a total emotional wreck and lucky that the people who chose to be with me understood that. Those dear friends let me be me. They did not take my emotions as a personal affront. They rode out my storm with me. I screamed in the shower and cried uncontrollably too at the seeming futility of life, the meaninglessness of small talk, television, and the frustration that life seems to go on, unchanged, for the sun and the birds.

I was enraged at those who were supposed to be helping me, like the funeral director and the banker, that they could not fix what actually was so very wrong. Yet I was depending on them to help me. Every little incompetence on their part drove me to utter frustration.

Confusion may be a part of other dealings as you try to balance accepting the death and wanting it never to have happened. You may appreciate the attention of friends yet push them away. You may not trust that the people with whom you are close will be there for you. (After all, your significant other "abandoned" you, no?) You may cling to your spouse's clothes at the same time you feel the need to empty the closet. You may sleep in his chair but cry every time you look at it and want it out of the house. You may want to spend time with her friends yet feel they are no longer part of your life. When you feel a touch of happiness over some innocent thing, like a deer in the yard, you may feel guilty and resent that small joy. All of this confusion and negativity will subside, but it does take time and the desire to heal.

Those who come to be with you, and those who wish they could but cannot, will most likely try to express their concern with WORDS. Even if the words are awkward, recognize that someone is reaching out to console you, You will hear some words that make you angry or more sad. Let those pass and believe that the speaker wanted to be kind. Words given in-person, by phone, by text, by email, by FaceBook or by regular mail are all expressions by those who care about you. Be comforted by them. Listen or read with an open receptive heart. I'm sorry for your loss was the simplest phrase that reassured me I was not alone emotionally. I especially appreciated people who were not very close to me offering that. Closer friends and family said "I'm sorry...I love you...I'm here for you" in more varied and meaningful ways. That someone was there to say "I love you" was very important and more so when coming from formerly reticent friends. Other helpful words were : *Be patient… be gentle with yourself…give yourself time …you'll learn to carry this…. things will change, it gets less despairing…you'll feel this way less frequently…you will always miss him… he'll be in your heart forever… love never dies… and grief is love with nowhere to go. One step at a time, one day at a time* and *he looked at you with such love* were particularly helpful words gleaned from sympathy cards, texts, and verbal communication

Closely following a death, anything longer than very short passages may challenge your concentration, yet in time reading words may be a huge comfort. Initially, I found short passages of a few lines helped me see some positives in life. You can seek words from others who have experienced grief and have survived. You can read about how they successfully processed their tragedy. You can read spiritual books that may help restore your spirit and point you in a positive direction by offering solace and strength.

Some spoken words may make you fall apart, setting off a deluge of grief. *Dead, widow, alone, the end, how, easy, better, odd one, third wheel, get over it, recover, and new life* are all words that can bring forth misery whether you hear them or simply feel them. Words that send you to a dark place can be released in the shower, without verbally attacking the well-intentioned person who offered them. The words you scream need to get out. Allowing yourself time alone to do whatever works to relieve your despair will help you to be patient with those who don't realize the effect that their words are having. Hopefully you will not be subjected to hurtful words, but if you are, deflect them; try to simply ask that they not be spoken or suggest a substitute word or phrase. *That's too painful now to talk about…Please…no,* or even a raised hand may suffice. Be patient with those who don't realize that the words they hope will be supportive or encouraging are sending you backwards into anger or despair.

Practice the other words you need to say comfortably and without hesitation. People will ask you, "What can I do?" Tell them! You might say: P*lease notify the others in our family, or the members of the Grange, or Book Club… Please post something on FaceBook, so my friends there know without my having to tell them… Come over and just hang out with me for a little while… Go with me to the bank or Social Security Office… Be here while I go through his closet… Come with me while I bury ashes… Help me figure out how to handle my bills… Come over while my grandkids are here and take them to have some fun-relief for an hour… Talk to me about having visitation and help me with invitations… Bring a blossom for a mixed bouquet… Send me the photos* *you have of us... Help me compose an email to notify his friends... Bring me dinner and just hang out with me for a while... Put his car on Craig's list for me, and handle the responses... Send your wife over... Call me each evening, or be available for my call... Just text me something encouraging every morning... Phone me occasionally and ask how I'm doing... Let me be emotional, cry or scream and then hug me anyway... Send or make something comforting: a plant, food, a pillow made of his shirt, a card with fond remembrances.* Whatever it s you need, speak up and ask!

Speaking with a close friend or counselor or taking part in group grief therapy sessions may provide the kind of processing that you need. You have suffered a trauma; it is extremely helpful to talk about it. A professional counselor can provide an objective sounding board to help you process what is happening within you, to debrief and finally move away from the death.

Words are integral to your thoughts and mental health. Reading, writing, music and audiovisuals each may or may not appeal to you. What you fill your head with is particularly important when grieving. It is likely that initially you'll be able to focus on such input from others for only a short time. What media you select depends upon your individual likes and dislikes; whatever it is, it should be positive. Choose carefully those inputs that make you feel better and practice directing your thoughts toward finding peace, bringing a smile, accepting, comforting, understanding, or even escaping.

You can bring comforting words and hugs closer by gathering together those family and friends who care about you and cared about the deceased Your background, religious or not, can determine when and how you do this. Planning such a function can help you focus on your loss in a constructive way.

I held visitation at our home soon after Ron's passing and later held a memorial service, a celebration of Ron's life, at his university. Design your choice to meet your own needs for support and sharing, and to accommodate the time and travel constraints of those you want to attend.

A friend of mine whose adult son passed away held visitations for three days before the funeral. Her home was open to those close to her and her husband to visit and express their sympathy with presence, hugs, food and voice. Her closest friends monitored her needs: sent guests to the table, living room or away; intercepted when the grieving parents needed time alone; tracked gifts for reference and thank you cards; and set out food, washed dishes and answered the door and phone.

Soon after the death, any celebration can seem off-putting. Celebration of life memorials can also surround you with care, understanding and reassurance that the deceased will not be forgotten. They are extremely helpful for those ready to cherish the memories of their loved one and who want those memories to continue to influence their life and the lives of their friends. Timing is of the essence; choose what fits your needs and desires, and chooses those whom you want to gather about you. The resources section of this book lists information about memorial types that serve as celebration of the deceased, as well as smaller more personal memorials.

Remember those who offer to help; they love you! Give them the gift of acceptance; give yourself that gift too. Be patient as you remember and forget, hold fast and let go; memorials of various types can help with that. Shiva, funeral, wake, visitation, celebration of life, burial, and scattering of ashes each can concurrently honor, hold the memory and say goodbye. They can serve as a step toward acceptance of the death, a formal way to say goodbye, a way to notify family and friends of the deceased, a way to recognize the anniversary date of his or her passing, and a way to gather those who would like to honor the deceased and offer mutual support to the survivors.

Activities totally different from your grief can be helpful too. Working for others in a way not connected with Ron became a safe harbor for me. I threw myself into creating a memorial movie for my mother about my dad. I forced myself to do what I saw as necessary duties for a club office that I held. I devoted time to a girlfriend in assisted living.

Friends who had also lost a spouse all chose something outside of their grief to focus on. One began teaching a sport as a necessary activity. Another took on working out on the courts with others as something that claimed her time much of the day. We all chose something outside of loss that demanded our time and mental focus.

Still mental focus on anything but loss was difficult. I found myself disorganized; formerly I was a very organized person. I became forgetful, unfocused, mentally blurry. To counteract that, I chose a volunteer activity that required being in the present moment… not much mental work but total focus. I devoted an afternoon each week to a Fire Corps, climbing ladders to replace smoke detector batteries for people no longer able to climb ladders, and capturing and moving rattlesnakes away from homes and public areas. Other times I concentrated on whatever situations my friends and family were in, helping them deal with lives that seemed, at that time, totally disconnected from mine.

## *Practices to Aid Communicating and Relating:*

Immediately following loss, you will focus mostly on the one you lost. Write him or her a letter, telling your most taboo responses to the death. If you are angry about his death, tell him! If you are lost without her, write about that. Whatever you are feeling, write it down to your beloved. Ask for his or her advice. Take care to address your feelings and relay them; then burn the letter sending it off in smoke to him or her.

**LETTER TO MY BELOVED** *(If you plan to burn this, give it its own pages!):*


Monitor your self-talk. Whatever you are thinking should be encouraging and healing. Write a few positive mantras to repeat frequently. (Eg: *I am strong; I am surviving this; I will smile each day; I will be kind to everyone I talk to; I have friends. My children, parents, siblings, community members need me.*) Post them on a mirror or wall where you will read them daily.

**MY DAILY POSITIVE MANTRAS:**

- 


- 


-

Communicating to others even the fact of your loved one's passing can be very trying. The Preface has pointed out necessary and early practical communications. Social media can greatly aid this, as can obituaries and services. Each of these can be researched on line. (See Appendix). Celebrations of life and participation in Day of the Dead are usually delayed to later phases of grief, so I will describe them in Phase II. Initially, the "celebration" aspect can feel improper. Early on, sitting shiva, holding visitations, or having a wake and funeral can surround you with care and understanding while you are feeling especially fragile.

***MY PUBLIC MEMORIALIZING THIS YEAR WILL BE:***

-

# *Guidepost I-C: Strengthening and Evolving Spiritually*

God, church, the Bible, and nature all can provide consolation to those with faith that life is not over, that life always holds love and goodness. You may have faith and draw upon it or search as I did to uncover faith. Receive the messages *Be Kind* and *Love One Another as Yourself*. Focusing on developing spirit can mesh spirit with emotions, thoughts, and action. For me that involved silent walks in nature, meditating, reading, time in church, and time as an introvert yet still connecting to others. Just being in the presence of what nourished my soul was healing. Such places, places you know as your true home, can surround and support you. Seek them.

Initially, dreams, imaginings, attachment to jewelry or other talisman, and signs can also provide much spiritual comfort. Many bereft people look for signs that their loved one still exists on some plane. I was fascinated to read that this is because the deceased still exists in the subconscious. That it is to be expected. Your loved one inhabited mental space, mental energy. Your neurons fired over and over, perhaps for decades, as you considered what he or she was doing, wanting, and planning. Whether you were together or not, somewhere in the back of your mind you held thoughts about when you'd next interact, what care was to be given, what food shared, what the emotional and physical response to each other would be.

The neural pathways still fire in the old way; for some that may continue for years. During that time you may find yourself looking for signs that the deceased still exists. You may expect him to come home at any minute, even though you know he cannot. You may see her in a flower. You may try to make contact through a medium or seance. One friend saw her husband in the form of a cardinal, his favorite bird, visiting the kitchen window every morning.

Another ascribed magical powers to numbers and to a song the memory of which brought back her husband. You may see your loved one appear on the street or in a doorway... at times then materialized into a stranger, at times to simply disappear. You may hear him talking or even feel his touch.

Photographs may be a spiritual comfort for you, bolstering you with images of your loved one or they may be an anchor pulling you down to despairing that he or she is no longer present. Let your actions be determined by your emotional response. Many bereft people pack away photographs of their beloved because they elicit pain; many others pour over albums and share photographs at memorial services in order to feel comfortable surrounded by the spirit of the departed.

Cremated remains can also cause spiritual comfort or distress. Again, let your own reaction dictate how you deal with them. Choices include permanently placing them in a grave or wall, encasing them in an urn or other container at your home and to be moved at will, scattering or burying them at significant locations, and a combination of these choices. Usually there is no need to decide immediately. Allow yourself time to feel assured that you are making the right choice for you.

You may find yourself talking to your spouse, may even hear responses, or see signs that indicate responses. Such things are normal and helpful to indulge in. Letters written to your deceased loved one or others particularly involved in the passing, can also be comforting, as can sending those letters to the spirit world in a column of smoke. Some bereft people set a place at the table for their late spouse or think of her when they visit favorite haunts. Take comfort in recognizing that these are ways to hold onto the deceased; they will gradually fade to belong to the after-life.

I found solace in spaces that I had not recently visited: church, music (Brahms' Requiem was especially healing), households of a brother seldom seen in adulthood and those of friends I had seen less of since my marriage.

During the first year or more, I awoke despairing that Ron was gone, and I had to re-set my mind to be open to positive experiences in a new day. I became intentional in how to BE each day: calm or industrious; thoughtful, kind; adventurous; open to sympathy; business-like…whatever my expectations of the day called for.

Another needed focus for me to take baby steps in forming a life without Ron was short text. Daily readings of just a page or less such as in *The Daily Word* and *How to Heal a Grieving Heart* served me well in the early months in regaining my spirit and finding a life without my spouse. They steered my thoughts and feelings in a positive hopeful direction away from pervasive grief. A bit later I found short entries into a nightly gratitude journal to be helpful. Gradually longer readings and entries were useful.

Readings from the Bible were one source that helped me take comfort by living what is important. A daily phone call to my mother (who needed me to be positive and had no idea that Ron had "relocated") helped me. I read postings on index cards and sheets of paper that I'd placed for myself throughout the house. One was a response I had written to my counselor's question of "Why are you still here?" I posted that I was

still here to…

> *Take part in life with my friends and family members and NOT distress them, not cause them the wrenching grief I've been feeling…*

> *Respect and honor Ron, what he gave me and what he gave the world, how well he provided for me, (this should continue so as to reach his kids and grandkids) and his years of love and consideration.*

> *Appreciate the world…particularly the God-given natural world. (I believe "appreciation is the key to happiness" ).*

> *Appreciate, use and contribute my own God-given talents and abilities.*

*Grow spiritually to better love my neighbor and love myself.*

*Grow spiritually to become a more solid sole person (ie in the role of self as independent from roles of wife, partner, daughter, mother, grandma) who is better able to recognize when I am deferring to others.*

*Accept and learn to carry grief, and recognize and appreciate that it began with love. "*

I'd daily read that posting for weeks. Also for weeks, before going to sleep at night, before crawling into those bedclothes alone, a phone call with my sister and a prayer of gratitude were essential to my peacefulness.

Consider that you are in the throes of immediate loss. Take all the time you need to deal with the practical matters that demand attention and the emotional acceptance that loss requires. The practices below as well as resources used in Phase I are potential choices to aid your ability to accept and carry this loss.

## *Practices to Aid Strengthening and Evolving Spiritually:*

Choose guidance to develop your spirit and spend some time with it. Choices include talking to your minister, reading the Bible, praying, meditating, listening to healing music, spending time in Nature, spending time with your most loving relative or friend...or whatever feeds your soul.

### *I'LL FEED MY SOUL DAILY BY:*

- 

Write your spouse another letter, this time telling about the love you shared and what you are thankful for. Burn the letter in a ceremony sending it off to him or her.

### *A SECOND LETTER TO MY BELOVED*

- 

Select a book (the Bible may work for you) with short encouraging passages such as *How to Heal a Grieving Heart*, (Virtue and Praagh, Hay House, Inc. 2013). You may prefer television, the internet, or other media, but access regular positive input to draw you back to the world of the living. What you fill your head with is particularly important after such a loss. Your individual likes and dislikes will determine what you are open to. Whichever it is, it is likely you'll be able to focus only for a short time. Record your form of positive input to draw you back into the world of the living.

***POSITIVE INPUT SELECTION AND NOTES:***

- 

You may have a strong relationship with your god; if so, write to God, and pray for what you hope for.

- 


***MY PRAYER/HOPES:***

- 


Consider a memorial and begin planning it. While immersed in early grief you will want to hold on to your loved one. Memorials of various types are ways to hold and share memories. Would you like to hold a lone memorial by writing and reading to your spouse a thank you letter, placing flowers on the grave, praying about her, burning clothing or other possessions, lighting a candle, setting a place at the table, sleeping in his chair, visiting a favorite haunt, or other familiar experience? Do it! Many bereaved people find this sort of thing healing.

*MY PRIVATE WAYS TO MEMORIALIZE:*

- 



*Be* gentle with yourself as you recover from shock. Allow yourself plenty of time to sleep intermittently throughout the day as you process what has happened and what must be done. Allow yourself time to scream in the shower. Push yourself to exercise, or at least to go for a walk. Suspend worries about the lives of those who do not need your care and allow them to become caregivers to you. Focus on helping those who are also grieving, particularly children you may have. Mutual support is healing. Time is healing. Post short reminders to yourself that help you stay pointed in the right direction. You might remind yourself to call the funeral home, to take your medications, to be kind, to offer a prayer of thanks each evening, to talk with Junior about the loss.

*REMINDERS FOR SELF CARE AND DIRECTION*

-

REMINDERS FOR MYSELF:

*PRACTICE I : YOUR MEDITATIVE COMPANION*

*It's Nature by God; Photos by Holly Chorba;*

*Words by Various Others*

**REMINDER**

*Appreciate the world;*

*particularly the God-given natural world.*

*Immerse yourself in peace and beauty.*

*Know that appreciation is the key to happiness.*

*(Chorba, 2001)*

**NATURE BY GOD**

## *SCREAM IN THE SHOWER*

**Scream in the shower**

**Howl at the moon. Retreat to your Bower.**

**Peace will come soon. Wrap up in her dress,**

**Sleep in his chair.**

**Feel the caress**

**of a spirit still there.**

**(Chorba, 2021)**

FULL MOON OVER AGAVES

## *BE*

*Sprawl on the ground in the woods*

*Roll onto your back*

*Look up at the sky*

*Relax, fall back into the arms of the earth*

*Take several deep breaths, slowly in and out*

*Imagine you are becoming part of the earth, that there are grasses and flowers growing out of the ground, right through your body*

*Feel the earth breathing under you, sighing with its moist scents*

*Feel the earth's heartbeat, its pulse*

*Feel the earth rotating, slowly turning east, away from the sun*

*Watch the clouds, feel the earth, read the cloud stories.*

*Directions to BE from Diana in "Blind your Ponies"*

*(West, 2001)*

**BE PART OF EARTH**

## *PATIENCE, THIS TOO WILL PASS*

*Wait!*

*Just be.*

*Don't plan.*

*Take care of the present; try not to orchestrate the future.*

*Be patient, kind, and gentle.*

*Deal with now.*

*"Stop trying to work things out before their time has come."*
*(Young, p.92)*

*"…in me you may have peace."*

*(John:16:33)*

NOW…THE BEAUTY OF BRIEF BLOSSOMS

## *I MOURN AND SO I SHOULD.*

*Grief is Love with nowhere to go.*

*You don't get over such a loss; you learn to carry it.*

*One step at a time; one day at a time.*

*Share your grief openly with those who allow it.*

*Be gentle, affirm the relationship, honor the soul.*

*Recognize and appreciate that grief began with love.*

*Believe in the positive possibilities.*

**NOWHERE TO GO**

You have contemplated the readings and writings of the Preface and Phase I, Immediate Loss. You are surviving grief. Initial devastation has calmed, perhaps numbness has set in. Return as often as it is helpful to ponder the headway you are making on your journey, shepherded by the guideposts. Use them to bolster yourself as needed. When you feel you are ready to progress in your life without your partner, continue navigating guided by this book.

Phase II of "It's Okay…Scream in the Shower" addresses regaining your balance. The text arrangement is the same: Physical and Emotional Well-Being, Communicating and Relating, and Strengthening and Evolving Spiritually, with Practices and Meditations embedded in each section. Phase II is an atlas to contemplate and guide your choices as you gain mental steadiness and emotional stability. Along your grief journey, continue caring for yourself and promoting self-healing You may want to explore the resources in the Appendix, return to Phase I and your thoughts or journal about it, or meditate more on the beauty that life still holds. When you are ready, continue reading Phase II. You will learn to carry grief; it will be an important part of love in your life. Listen to yourself and proceed gently in your own time.

# PHASE II
# REGAINING YOUR BALANCE

### TODAY

*Look to this day*
*For it is the very life of life.*
*In its brief course lie all the verities and realities of your existence:*
*The glory of action,*
*The bliss of growth,*
*The splendor of beauty.*
*For yesterday is but a dream and tomorrow only a vision.*
*But today well lived makes every yesterday a dream of happiness*
*and every tomorrow a vision of hope.*
*Look well therefore to this day. (Anonymous)*

**LOOK WELL TO THIS DAY!**

# *Guidepost II- A:*
# *Physical and Emotional Being*

The day will come (today?) when you begin to feel like an entire person again. Oh, you still will be grieving; you still will be drawn to thinking about your lost loved one, almost constantly; but you will do that less. Recover the thoughts, attitudes and behaviors that served you as an individual. Turn from thinking about the circumstances of the death and the days immediately preceding it. Focus on living in the present, today.

## *Practices:*

Still, in nearly two years after my devastating loss, I found that it's MORE than OKAY TO SCREAM IN THE SHOWER!…it's advisable! It is a way to reclaim yourself! GRIEVE; it is all that makes sense for you right now. Accept your emotions. Choose a way to release them, whether it is to scream in the shower, cry in the closet, clean the house with vengeance, or jog for miles. Find a release that works for you.

**I RELEASE MY EMOTIONS BY:**
- 

Recognize (as you regain living the reality of what exists now) that once it is tomorrow, today is gone. Re-read the poem *TODAY* at the beginning of this phase; consider posting it to read daily. Utilize that or another method to draw yourself from the past.

**I WILL FOCUS ON THE PRESENT, ON TODAY, BY:**
- 


**I ACKNOWLEDGE MY ACCEPTANCE OF DEATH BY:**
- 


Time does pass. You will find yourself gradually living more in the present, accepting that your beloved is indeed no longer on earth. At the same time you may become more aware and more accepting that life is temporary for all of us. You may find as you recognize that, your heart still beats, your senses still take in the present, and your brain perceives life further out from you, that loss continues and you don't control your life. Two years from Ron's death I wrote to a friend, "Yes, still grieving, but I am okay". Grief is almost separate now. It is there, ever present, yet apart from the present. I still wish Ron had lived, wish somehow I could have prevented his passing, but I recognize that his death happened and cannot be changed. Death happens. We might sometimes think we can delay it, but we cannot avoid it entirely. It has been months since my mother died, a year before that, Ron died and three years before, Dad died. Now the Corona Virus is taking the lives of thousands, and my friend Carol is dying in Hospice Care. Death is a fact of life.

Ellen, who lost her husband 1 1/2 years before Carol's illness, says those more current losses bring back the grief of the earlier passings. We are losing our friend Carol; we are still mourning the losses of our husbands and others. We are more susceptible to loneliness and negativity. We need to revisit our earlier means of handling grief.

Remember to pay attention to your physical self. Time passes, aging happens, your health is most likely affected by grief. Consider whether your sleep and dietary habits have returned to normal, whether you are taking any prescribed medications on schedule, or whether your anxiety level has changed. Work away the extra physical tension you may have. Make that doctor's appointment if you are not feeling healthy. Grooming is another aspect that, initially, those bereft may ignore. Get back to it! Believe that you should take care of yourself in these basic, personal ways. Gradually, you will get comfortable wearing what you wore previously, or with a new self-image.

Chances are that your life with your dearly departed was centered in a house that had become your home, and a bed that had become your marriage. Early on, after loss, you may need to either get out of the house, to escape the fact that your spouse is no longer there, or you may need to stay in the house, just in case he or she somehow magically comes home. Gradually, in either case, that will change to acceptance, and you will begin to realize that you are living alone in that house. You may learn to be comfortable by making that house your *home alone* or you may find that *home* is where your heart is now; perhaps you will find it necessary to change that place to somewhere else.

If you are like Ellen, you will absent yourself much of the day, socializing with friends; if you are like me, you will find others to live in the house with you. It's the same thing…buffering yourself from the aloneness that is different from loneliness. It is more the shock from missing half of yourself, to which you need to adapt.

The *home* aspect of your house may gradually change too… eventually you accept that the details that made it a home either still belong now to you alone (and therefore make it YOUR home), or are artifacts of a past that has passed. You may happily live with the dining room set you loved for entertaining, but eventually send the clothes and chair that belonged to your wife to Good Will. For some this might take days or weeks, for others it might take years. While in early mourning, I slept in my husband's lounge chair for hours every dawn. Time passed, and I spent less sleeping time in that chair and eventually gave it to charity. Rest assured, you will eventually accept that your loved one no longer needs such personal possessions. Chairs, clothes and many useful items can do more good when given to others.

You may find your need to be physically close to other people is satisfied by your normal living arrangement, or you'll find that modifications are needed. Common ones include: moving near a child or sibling; having long term house guests; selling your home and moving to smaller, less secluded housing; entering a group living arrangement; finding a friend or relative to move in with you; or getting a pet for company. Your age and financial situation have a big effect on which you choose. Choose what you can afford and what you are comfortable with in the present.

Your marriage bed is another physical artifact of your joint life that may be laden with emotion. After 20 months I was still sleeping with a pillow made from my husband's shirts; I still usually slept in one of his tee shirts. His half of the bed was still filled with bolsters and a teddy bear. I even borrowed a friend's dog to sleep with me!

The physical aspect of marriage of course also disappears, and is more likely to manifest itself as an unmet need. I found I greatly missed the sexual contact; it was part of the grief, connected with missing Ron, not with desire for anyone else.

Your libido may simply be non-existent for a time…for months, or perhaps for some people, for years. It may depend on the status of your marriage. Were you active? Were you dormant and "coasting" into some non-sexual phase due to illness, age, whatever? Were you like me before grief overcame you, alive and well and enjoying an active sexual relationship, an affirmation that life itself is orgasmic?

Many months after losing Ron, I had begun to feel a sexual tension; the urge to fulfill that basic need was causing me more stress; something I definitely didn't need. It helped me to hunker down in the privacy and security of my own home and marriage bed and do something myself to quell that. I was not particularly well versed in how to do this, but like all sex it's something you can experiment with and get better at. Talking with friends can provide information; TV shows like *Sex and the City* and magazines like *Mademoiselle* can too. Some friends turned to others soon after bereavement to quench their sexual needs. They invariably found that the resulting emotional and physical complications caused more stress.

So, for me, physical and emotional desires were at first limited to self-expression. It was too precarious to involve myself closely with the opposite sex. Grief and the threat of another loss overcame any desire to connect. You may feel this way, for a time or forever. You may want to connect closely again and be open to a significant other or not!

Home and bed for many, including me, gradually lost its hold, and my desire to mix with society and travel took over my desire to hold fast to the past. At first I ventured alone to the grocery store, gas station, a park or to club meetings. My "saviors" drove me across the country to my summer home; to the house I truly considered *home*. Adjusting to being without Ron re-emerged and dependence on others rose. I relied on a brother to accompany me to appointments at places such as the Social Security Office, and then down the coast to visit our mother. I took short day trips alone; I met up with groups, although I found I could not tolerate being in large groups. I needed more of a close connection to those individuals I interacted with and the opportunity to withdraw a bit from any group. After 4 months I managed a car trip around the state; after six months, I flew back down the coast for my mother's birthday and to visit my in-laws. This time I was able to travel alone!

Time, experience, acceptance, and forging a new life gradually take hold. Mourning emotions are temporary; be patient with yourself. Allow time to heal. You will! Raw emotion becomes less intense. You will need to sleep less, to nap less often, to absent yourself from the present less, and to scream in the shower less frequently, and with less intensity. Dawn will illuminate your life.

## *Practices to Aid Physical and Emotional Being:*

Share your thoughts and emotions with another. (See Chapter 6, *Rupture* of *Pussy: A Reclamation*, Regena Thomashauer, Hay House Inc. 2016). Seek emotional and physical support from doctors, counselors, grief groups, a close friend or friends. What is important is that you have an outlet for sharing what you are going through. You may need a physical, medical advice or medication to help you get the sleep you need. Some people reject drug therapy; some fit it in to their normal life style; some accept it during exceptional circumstances. If you choose drug therapy, you should be monitored by a professional who is objective and can observe your reactions.

**I CHOOSE TO SHARE MY THOUGHTS AND EMOTIONS WITH:**
- 

**I ADDRESS MY PHYSICAL SYMPTOMS, INCLUDING SLEEP PATTERNS AND LIBIDO BY:**
-

Consider your gratifying roles in life and get back to them, whether they be to: facilitate, support, teach, create, produce, or share mutual enjoyment. Did you enjoy the role of teacher, parent, business leader, administrator, first responder, minister, farmer, care-giver, housekeeper, builder, coach, artist, or sports participant? Choose roles most similar to ones that you delighted in. Get active again in such activities. Recognize the help, love and belonging you've recently experienced and combine that with roles you can now participate in. Commit to them and get going!

**I FIND FEELINGS OF HOME IN :**
- 

**I PARTICIPATE WITH OTHERS BY:**
-

# *Guidepost II-B: Communicating and Relating*

*Look to others…BE KIND!*

The friends who stuck by me tolerated my initial emotional overload. That I was distraught and out of control soon became NOT okay with me. The storm had kept building instead of subsiding. I was allowing myself to continue being distraught, feeding my own distress. Gradually I sensed that I was out of control, upsetting others. I realized that I did not want to cause the very people who were there to console me the distress that I was feeling. That was one of the realizations that saved me from myself !

I forced myself to regain my emotional balance and took my cues from my supporters on how to look at life. I directed myself to be considerate of others including notifying people of Ron's death, making arrangements for memorials, and holding services. I knew others were grieving also, and it was up to me to provide comfort and hugs, virtual and in-person. As with any hugs, those hugs were mutual. Months had passed when I recalled a scene from Ken Follett's *Pillars of the Earth* and recognized that connection with life can bring one back from the brink of despair. Find your connection to your present life! Choices include: taking care of your children, parents, or pets; work (if still employed, pour yourself into it!); if retired, consider taking on a volunteer job; remodel your home; research other lifestyles and places to live; hug your teddy bear, a pillow made of your spouses clothes, or even your favorite tree; enjoy get togethers or slumber parties with siblings or friends; engage in your favorite physical activity such as pickle ball, tennis, or gardening; immerse yourself in treks in nature; meditate in a cathedral;

cultivate new friendships. Whatever connects you with this earth, do it. Your spouse has relocated, and it's best not to relocate yourself. You are not done on this earth! Sample a path or two alone!

As time goes on, staying close to the deceased, and to those close to him or her, needs to be countered with also moving away. Working for others in a way not connected with Ron became a safe harbor for me. I threw myself into creating movies to capture other important people and places in my life. I forced myself to do what I saw as necessary duties for a club office that I held. I devoted time to people in assisted living, entertaining them with my movie productions and photo classes. I donated clothing and furniture to friends and charities. Find your way to give of yourself to those in need.

Friends who had also lost a spouse all chose something outside of their grief to focus on. One began (as a now-necessary activity for her) teaching a sport. Another took on working out at the gym with others as something that demanded her time most of the day. One devoted herself to work through her church. One sewed clothes for needy children. We all chose something outside of loss that demanded our time and mental focus.

Your receptivity to certain words and thoughts will also change as time passes. Thinking of forming a n*ew life* at first was intolerable. After 15 months, that phrase was hopeful and thought provoking. (The same held true for *You are strong*; *You have good resources; We are survivors!*) Some words at times still evoked an over-emotional response. Finding words that were less unsettling helped me deal better with others and think in a less distressed manner. They helped me accept Ron's *passing*. (My sister-in-law who had found a phrase less upsetting to her nursing home patients, offered *He's relocated* as an alternative to *He died*.) *Take one step at a time… You will learn to carry grief…* were all more encouraging than *It's time you move on*.

When talking business to others, I had cried every time I told a vendor that my husband had *died*. A friend suggested that I use instead, *I lost my husband*, and I found I could tolerate relaying that. Keep in mind that everyone seeks a new balance differently. Many people with whom you'll deal have no idea of your loss; you can make the choice of which words to use and which to avoid.

Normal situations and pastimes may be intolerable for you too. Initially, television was that for me; after 16 months I was still avoiding it. At first small talk also sent me into orbit; later I could accept it as normal behavior, though small talk has never been something I enjoy.

Reading words can be a comfort. Longer reads eventually became possible and helpful to me. You can read how others who have experienced grief have survived. You can read about how they processed their tragedy. You can read spiritual books that may help you restore your soul, point you in a positive direction, or offer solace. A counselor or group sessions may provide encouraging source material or similar support through speaking and discussion.

Timing is important. Offerings like "I know of a great singles group that you may enjoy" or "Why don't you come to dinner? John will be there; he lost his wife two years ago," may be welcome after YOU have decided that you are open to new relationships, but certainly are not when you are in the throes of grief. When those words are offered prematurely, recognize that the speaker is hoping that someday you will participate in life more normally even though now is not the time for you.

Remember as you move away from the focus on bereavement, that it's still okay to *SCREAM IN THE SHOWER*. It's still okay to visit Phase I. No one would want to live there forever; it's emotionally wrenching. So visit that shower stall or special place when you need. Words that send you to a dark place can be released there, without attacking the kindness of the person who unwittingly offered them. The words that you scream need to be released. Allow yourself to do whatever works to relieve the intensity of your despair. Everyone seeks a new balance differently. Be patient with those who don't realize that the words they hope will be supportive or encouraging are sending you backwards into darkness. Let them go and look for light.

Your receptivity to hugs may change as well. Perhaps initially you welcomed (even needed) hugs, especially from family. Hugs from near strangers who attend a memorial for your significant other may also be welcome. Time passes, surroundings change, and your perception of hugs may change . A hug from a stranger may be interpreted as an unwelcome advance. Maybe the interest is appropriate, just premature. Only you can decide that, and you need to recognize that he or she may not be trying to threaten you or come-on to you. Your take depends on your personal space boundaries and your sense of intent.The women I know who have lost a beloved husband have particular difficulty interpreting support from male friends. Emotions are running high and easily confused. A hug may seem supportive and be welcome or seem more of a sexual come-on and elicit alarm, resentment, even anger. There may be a perceived sexual component to consolation, especially between close friends, which can be misleading on both parts. Don't be surprised if your reaction to the opposite sex is extreme.

Other grieving people might turn to "friends with benefits" as a means to be comforted sexually without the threat of a new, strange, potentially emotionally charged relationship, not to mention the threat of another loss. Hugs can awaken a need for more physical contact and comfort. You may find that you miss the physical contact and comfort of your spouse. There are words from a song, "people who need people are the luckiest people in the world" and sex with oneself does not quite satisfy. So, you weigh the protection from emotional involvement, protection from another potential loss, and potential exposure to STDs against biology, latent sexuality and the desire for intimacy.

Maybe you'll find someone to fulfill your sexual needs; maybe you will resolve to remain true to your late spouse; maybe you have no sexual desire and will keep that status as is. The world is full of widows and widowers who make such choices. Time, experience, your own make-up, fate, and luck will determine which road you take.

Psychologically, you determine your fate. My dad used to say, "Good luck is when preparation meets opportunity. When opportunity knocks, open the door!" Whatever notions you adopt will prepare you for a life that includes sexual love (or not) or that includes the potential to have an intimate partner (or not). You do control your thoughts. Pay attention! Another truism I've embraced is to *be careful what you wish for, for you shall surely get it*. Believe that you can find another, albeit different, significant mate to love, and it can happen.

The Preface ends with:

> *See friends, take classes, keep up with your activities. You have a lot of life left in you and hubby would want you to live it. Go out for lunch and dinner. Talk about your husband; your friends loved him too and want to reminisce about the good times. Cry when you have to, but don't get lost in it. Say good night to him every night.*
>
> *Don't be surprised if you can't stand to cook for one, don't want to eat and, lose weight. The day may come when anything not moving looks good to eat and you gain all the weight back. Don't be surprised if it's almost impossible to do alone the things you used to do with him. Find a hobby you didn't share with him.*
>
> *Expect it to take a long time for complete recovery. You'll think you're fine and then months later fall into a well of despair. Climb out. Get moving, do*

*something. Don't expect to tick off the 7 stages of grief—you may miss quite a few of them and find your very own stage or two.*

*Linda Sparks, (2009)*

I found these words very helpful as I began to regain my balance. Reread the Preface, apply its encouragement as your mental and emotional states allow. You will likely incorporate the spirit of your loved one into your present and future life. You may also incorporate into your life some of his or her family, friends and objects…photos, tools, clothes, furniture…things that fit your present circumstances and bring back happy memories.

You may feel the need to hold on to the past while grasping for the present; you may feel great sympathy for anyone experiencing loss, and want to reach out to them. I did. I felt the need to write this book and share it as an offering to you, someone who is hurting from loss of a significant other. This started first as a journal to help me remember my being as I struggled with my own loss. Sometimes that was comforting to me, sometimes I needed to get away from it for weeks, and later, for months. Earlier on, the writing and remembering brought back the rage that Ron was gone, the pain that he had passed and that I could not control that. As time went on I realized that I had to accept grief as part of me, but not all of me. I also had to accept life as part of me…the reality of the here and now (without Ron on earth) and the possibilities of my future here. Possibly a happy future…I had and have much to live for, much to love for.

At times I still am washed over by a desire to quit, or with regret that I did not control and cannot control death. I've come to terms with accepting that is how life is, how it is for everyone, how it has always been, and to thank God for the many blessings in this life. Most of the time my grief resides on a shelf, and I know in my soul that life, loss, and grief are all part of the truth of our existence.

Several friends had advised counseling. I had been neglecting my spiritual aspect and I recognized I needed to have help handling my more destructive tendencies. Negativity kept sneaking into my psyche, magnifying every little mistake or insensitivity toward me by those who were focused on their own inheritance and grief, their own take on how Ron had conducted his life, and their own fear of the impending deaths of their loved ones.

I wanted to regain my loving, more forgiving self, and I believed I'd understand the world including trauma and loss much better through the objective eyes of a counselor. It took me a few tries to find a good match, a counselor whom I found helpful and who believed that she could help me. Robin did. She was an objective, confidential sounding board who helped me ferret out when I was being over-emotional and when I needed to unload sadness. I answered her questions of "What has kept you here… after four months, you are still with us… why?" I printed out my answers and posted them on my office wall to help me maintain focus and anchor myself to the present. Contemplate your own reasons, and read mine again:

*So… I'm here to:*

*Take part in life with my friends and family members and NOT distress them, not cause them the wrenching grief I've been feeling;*

*Respect and honor Ron, what he gave me and the world, how well he provided for me, (this should continue to reach his kids and grandkids) his years of love and consideration;*

*Appreciate the world…particularly the god-given natural world (I believe that appreciation is the key to happiness);*

*Appreciate, use and contribute my own god-given talents and abilities;*

*Grow spiritually to better love my neighbor, even love myself;*

*Grow spiritually to become a more solid sole person (as in the role of self, apart from wife, partner, daughter, mother, grandma) who is better able to recognize when I'm deferring;*

*Accept and learn to carry grief, and appreciate that it began with love.*

I became more positively other-directed and connected with important events happening in others' lives, like my friend Donna's retirement and my grandson's graduation. I practiced being happy for them. I cooked, shared my house, crafted experiences, hugged and shared thoughts. I recognized the caring of friends and the caring of God via Nature. I was grateful for what talents and abilities I had. I celebrated that I still could see beauty in Nature. I still could taste good food, my sister still could make me laugh and Ron's spirit still could give me good advice. I was grateful for a brain that could think about thinking. I was thankful for what patience I had, for the new-born fawn I saw two days ago, for brother Dean's inscribing Ron's memorial rock, friend Marcy's cooking for me, brother Frank's looking out for me and accompanying me to business meetings, Maureen's communicating, and Heather and William's visiting.

I limited the amount of time that I allowed myself to mourn, obsess about losing Ron and worry about the future. I wrote nightly in a "Gratitude Journal" those things and others I was thankful for.

I resolved to pretend that I was okay most of the day…it helped! I began starting each day with a meditation followed by thinking about how I would BE that day… calm, loving, caring, diligent, focused or whatever I felt was called for to serve the present.

Set limits for when you allow mourning; limit obsessing about your loss and worrying about the future. Some find it useful to actually dedicate a particular hour of the day for mourning and the remainder to getting on with life.

Find positive inputs for yourself. Memorials that are held months, or even years after a loss can steer your thoughts of the past in a positive direction. You likely will want your significant other's life somehow to remain, and to continue to be part of, those who loved him or her.

Memorials such as *Celebration of Life, Dia de los Muertos,* and *Parade of the little Angels* gather these people and celebrate the spirit of the deceased. (See Appendix.) Personally crafted celebrations might include: burial or scattering of ashes; release of balloons, birds or butterflies; review of photos or home movies; prayers at the grave and writing and burning of letters to the deceased.

# Practices to Aid Communicating and Relating:

You will regain your emotional balance. Choose something outside your grief to connect you with others.

**I EXPRESS MY PRESENT FOCUS ON OUTSIDE INTERESTS BY:**
- 

**I GIVE OF MYSELF TO THOSE IN NEED BY:**
- 

**I RECOGNIZE MY OVER-EMOTIONAL RESPONSE TO CERTAIN WORDS OR SITUATIONS AND COMPENSATE BY:**
- 

**NOW MY RESPONSE TO A POTENTIAL PARTNER IS:**
-

**I RECOGNIZE MY CONFUSION AS EVIDENCED BY THIS BEHAVIOR:**
- 


**I RELY ON THE FOLLOWING MEANS ( journaling, counseling , escape to television, books, sports, travel, moving) TO HELP ME HEAL:**
- 


**I CRAFT THIS POSITIVE APPRECIATIVE CEREMONY TO CELEBRATE MY SIGNIFICANT OTHER'S LIFE BY:**
- 


Travel: Go toward something you see as positive, be it to enjoy a change of scene, be with friends who have recovered from loss, celebrate an event or holiday with friends, or re-connect with someone.

**MY TRAVEL WILL BE TO GO TO:**
-

# *Guidepost II-C:*
# *Strengthening and Evolving Spiritually*

*Recognize Mortality: LET GO; LET GOD*

### SERENITY PRAYER

*God,*
*Grant me the*
*SERENITY to accept the things I cannot change,*
*COURAGE to change the things I can, and*
*WISDOM to know the difference.    (Reinhold Niebuhr)*

As you seek spiritual solace, you could take in more and more information and energy from outside yourself through reading, the internet, television, and listening to others. Months after I was first bereft, I read many books about grief. I was intent on trying to discover ways to deal with being so distraught that I was beside myself. Initially, I could only focus on books written in short passages and offering a few lines or paragraphs per day that pointed my mind in a positive direction. While regaining my balance, I became more interested in how others grieved, how they learned to carry loss, how I might do that myself and how I could regain my spirit. Put yourself in the company of authors or producers you can relate to, ones who reach out through their work to give a hand up. (See Appendix for suggestions.)

You will begin to realize that though you do have a future, the mirage of control of your life is gone. I lost that mirage when Ron died. I wanted control. I wanted Ron back. I wanted all our dreams and plans to go on. Many of those dreams and plans went up in smoke. *Let go, let God* in order to find peace; accept that you do not control what tomorrow brings.

Thoughts and memories sometimes lead to despair over loss. Refocus on loving the present, loving your neighbor and yourself, turning away from pain, distress, blame, anger, outrage and jealousy. Focus instead on the present, on becoming a sole-soul. Recognize that you are getting older (We all are!) Recognize that you are going to die (We all are!) Not yet, but someday. Life will end; sorrow, joy, pain and happiness will end. It is up to you to accept the gift of life and to accept, respect, reconcile and cultivate current circumstances. Find your god and resolve yourself to a life without your former mate.

Writing in an expanded gratitude journal helps one appreciate life; writing daily intentions steers one toward this more positive outlook. Coach yourself to smile at each stranger, be kind to those who come to visit, graciously accept offers to help. Remind yourself that most everyone does the best that he or she can in order to think, talk, and act kindly. Remove yourself from anyone who does not. Remember to be patient and gentle with yourself and those who do offer solace.

Journal-writing helped me to reminisce about the good times that I had experienced with my husband and to realize how very lucky I was to have had those times. I loved how we had shared adventures in nature: Wilderness of Rocks, Happy Valley Saddle, The Northville-Placid Trail, and others. Ron cultivated my love of the back-country, paddling, and hiking. I also thanked him for being there during the rough times when I had lost my son, when I had breast surgery, when my father died. Usually such thoughts encouraged me to know that life had been good, even much better than many people ever experience. Those memories gave me confidence that I was lovable, that I could love life again, and that I could reach out for a different, yet happy, way of being. They also served to help me write a thank you letter to Ron, a eulogy to be shared at his memorial service.

After months or even years you may find yourself analyzing your past and your relationships with others, and then seeing a new or at least varied course that allows you to move away from the pain of grief, actually a reprieve from the painful past and toward increased satisfaction with present life. Communicate, love, forgive, accept, and make the most of what you have now.

Some of us, me for one, are psychologically changed by marriage or holding bonds with a significant other. After thirty years of marriage I was no longer *ME but WE*. *WE* manifests itself in various ways…what is subconsciously on your mind 24 hours a day, what activities you choose to do, what you eat, when you have a drink, whether you engage in a church, which friends you hang out with, and how you celebrate important events. The list goes on. When you are both retired, this aspect of life may become even greater. After a partner's death, the subconscious aspect of *WE* does not simply disappear. It stays on and on for months, maybe longer. You deal with that by setting a place at the table for your spouse, or buying her Christmas presents, or celebrating his birthday, or simply not being interested in sex, or wanting to stay home and be there if needed. You probably will think that you'll never marry again, that you are already (still) married, that even if you do become part of a couple, you really still belong with your late partner. It was the two of you who were meant for each other, and this death wasn't meant to happen. Whether I ever would want to or could unite somehow with a partner different from my late spouse, gradually became a potential possibility in my thoughts. I was and am comforted by the belief that love is forever, regardless of what the future may hold.

You may wonder whether you and your significant other can reunite in heaven. Alternately, some couples (like Romeo and Juliet) consider re-joining in death. I explored what my counselor and the Bible had to say about this issue. My counselor made me promise to wait, to not do myself in for at least a year, to write down why I was still on this earth. (You read previously my response, seven reasons I committed to for remaining on this earth for the near future.) I referred to it often. My more religious friends pointed me to the passage in the Bible (Matthew 22:23-34) that says those we see in heaven will be like angels, and the concept of marriage will not exist.

Consider that you are regaining your balance. Direct your thoughts and actions to life beyond grief; your emotions will follow. If and when you regress, re-direct your attention and thoughts to those people and activities that engage you. The practices below as well as the in the Appendix of this book offer suggestions to aid your Grief Journey.

## *Practices to Aid Strengthening and Evolving Spiritually :*

Contemplate how you are feeding your spirit. It is likely that you need to heal and evolve in order to accept the mortality, and even the life, of your lost love one and of yourself. You may find solace and guides through your faith, or even a borrowed faith, as well as through your sources of peace and satisfaction.

**I GET POSITIVE, SUPPORTIVE INPUT FOR MY SPIRIT FROM:**
- 

**I CELEBRATE THE GIFTS OF MY PAST LIFE WITH MY SPOUSE BY:**
- 

**I CULTIVATE AN ATTITUDE OF CELEBRATION AND GRATITUDE FOR MY CURRENT LIFE, MY PRESENT DAY, BY:**
- 

**I AM HERE ON THIS EARTH IN ORDER TO:**
-

# NOTES TO MYSELF:

## PRACTICE II WITH YOUR MEDITATIVE COMPANION
*It's Nature by God; Photos by Holly Chorba*

*Words by Various Others*

## Phase II, Regaining Your Balance

**REGAIN YOUR BALANCE**

## MEMORIALS

*I am sad and grieving.*

*I've lost the physical presence of my most important person.*

*I'd have to be someone else NOT to be sad, yet I am comforted by the spirit that still lives within me.*

*I have a way to hold that spirit close, to honor it and share it with friends and allow its joy to keep giving.*

*There is much good in my world, including this spirit.*

*I am surrounded by those we loved,*

*whom we cared for, who care for us.*

**HOLD THAT SPIRIT CLOSE**

## *NATURE, MUSIC, AND PRAYER*

*When negative emotions are triggered,*

*I shift to Nature, Music, and Prayer.*

*I deny the "pain body" of toxic thoughts and unwanted, unneeded emotions.*

*I deny feeling sorry for myself, defeatism, and worrying.*

*I sing the song "Accentuate the Positive." (Arlen and Mercer)*

*I cultivate a positive mood by listening to soothing music.*

*I cultivate a positive mood by immersing myself in nature.*

*I cultivate a positive mood through prayer,*

*focusing on gratitude, intentions and hopes.*

**IMMERSE IN NATURE**

*Trust in the Lord*

*Trust in the Lord*

*with all your heart*

*and lean not*

*on your own understanding.*

*(Proverbs 3:5)*

*Signs of MY Presence*

*brighten even the dullest day*

*when you have eyes that really see.*

*Search for Me as for hidden treasure.*

*I will be found by you.*

*("Jesus Calling" Young, p.93)*

**HIDDEN TREASURE**

*"In the end only three things matter:*

*how much you loved*

*how gently you lived and*

*how gracefully you let go*

*of things not meant for you."*

*(Banna Samerpitak)*


*Love God;*

*Love your neighbor as yourself.*

**YOU LOVED… GRACEFULLY LET GO**

You have progressed through "Phase II, Regaining your Balance". You are learning to navigate life, carrying grief with strength and stability. Continue to use all sections of *It's Okay…Scream in the Shower* as resources to help you navigate life without your partner. Re-read, peruse, add to your writings and meditate as you find fruitful.

Phase III of *It's Okay…Scream in the Shower* addresses life after loss. What does God have for you to do next? You may or may not believe in a god, the one I do, a different god, or any god at all. Your life, and your beliefs after all, are up to you. Your life carrying grief is up to you too. How much you shelve grief to a background vibration, how much positive or negative feeling you retain from your lost relationship and the trauma of losing it, and how much you turn to evolving your spirituality and entire life until death are all up to you.

Remember that *life is not a practice run. Life* (as we know it) *is temporary; you only have a finite time on this earth.*

The text arrangement of Phase III is the same: Physical and Emotional Well-Being, Communicating and Relating, and Strengthening and Evolving Spiritually, with Practices and Meditations embedded in each section. Phase III touches on issues that you probably did not anticipate facing, but that may well arise as you continue living. Phase III is short by design since as you experience the later issues of life without your partner those issues are less and less necessarily connected with death and grief. They are the issues single people of any circumstance face and which are addressed by a plethora of books about life itself.

# Phase III
# LIFE AFTER LOSS

*WHAT DOES GOD HAVE FOR YOU TO DO NEXT?*

*HAPPY TRAILS*

*Some trails are happy ones,*
*Others are blue.*
*It's the way you ride the trail that counts,*
*Here's a happy one for you. ...*

*Happy trails to you,*
*Until we meet again.*

*(Dale Evans)*

**HERE'S A HAPPY TRAIL FOR YOU!**

# PHASE III: LIFE AFTER LOSS

I realize as I am writing Phase III that I won't be able to fully complete this writing. Phase III is about living and loving, and my writing of it cannot last as long as I will. I've decided to move forward, to live again, to love again. This is a decision not every grieving person makes. You, I hope, will come to believe the old adage, *It's better to have loved and lost than never to have loved,* and apply it to your present. You will probably find it natural to first love those you did not lose, family and friends who are there for you. Gradually, you may open your heart to still love humankind in general and to love in new relationships. You may find, initially, that you reject love of God, because you direct anger at God for your loss. Or, you may you find you love God more than ever because you believe all the good you had and will have comes from God. Or, you may not believe in God, and think your loss was determined by factors in your control, or in someone else's, or because of luck. Whatever the cause you ascribe to your misfortune, seek acceptance and resolution of loss and set a direction shifting away from it.

It would be over two and one half years between Ron's passing and my resolve to absorb my experiences and coping mechanisms, finish my writing and give it forward to you, one who is also suffering the loss of a most significant person. Hopefully, you will have a continuing life that holds love and purpose, one which will bring you peace, contentment, and joy! It may have been difficult to even hope for such things when in the throes of grief, yet I have several friends who have found that is exactly how their life evolved. Some took eight years before they experienced that light, some a few years… two, just several months. Factors effecting that time include the qualities of the relationship you lost, your own spiritual life, your age and health, your social circumstances (including family and friends), your personality, your desire to connect with the living, your willingness to let go of grief, luck, fate and God's gifts to you.

# *Guidepost III-A: Physical and Emotional Being*

Allow yourself to be happy. Accept life as a part of you, accept the reality of the here and now without your loved one and the possibility of a future for you, a happy future! Sometimes your loss will still enter your psyche. You may feel totally distraught again. Make the effort to put that aspect of grief on a shelf. Direct your thoughts to use that grief as a way to hold and honor your late spouse…to recognize and rejoice in the significance of that relationship to you in the past, now, and forever. Hold the spirit of your lost loved one close as an enhancement of you and of your present life.

Friends and I who have experienced wrenching loss have found ways to commemorate our loved one years afterward. Keep the good memories alive, yet let go enough to move forward. Recognize the fact that loss is how life must be when the time comes, that is how it has always been, then thank God for giving you many blessings in life, past, present, and future. Focus on what you have to live for, what love you have to give and receive.

Your negative emotions will gradually subside. Words that once hurt will have less of an impact. Tears won't spontaneously arise nearly as often.

There began to be hours, then parts of days, then full days, when I felt myself returning from an altered state. That state was overwhelming grief. I gradually began to know what *learning to carry grief* means. Grief became a background vibration, evident less and less during the day and eventually less and less at night.

Grief now remains, mostly in my subconscious, a force within me to incorporate into my being. It reappears at holidays, anniversaries or when other close friends die. It is deja vu; the feelings return, but not with the intensity or duration as earlier. It helps me to use that grief to appreciate the positives of that previous relationship. They have become a part of me alone, of my sole soul. Establishing habits of allowing grief to feed my soul, to lead to my understanding of this world, to cultivate Ron's contributions to my existence as a positive aspect of who I am, all enhance my life.

You may find yourself becoming more stable emotionally. Outbursts will subside. You will very likely isolate less and feel more like taking part in the world around you. The return of emotional stability is accompanied by feeling more physically normal again. You'll begin to want to dress in your habitual manner, wear that jewelry that meant something other than loss, and even want to select new clothing and jewelry to reflect and support your current life. You may do the same with your home, house, and bed. This might be simply by redecorating: changing rooms around, posting and removing photos, buying a new bedspread, or using a different shower. It might be by moving entirely, selecting a different type of living arrangement such as an apartment in the city instead of a house in the country or a condo instead of a house.

You will probably want to incorporate other people into your life more than at the time of initial loss. Reach out and remember; *People who need people are the luckiest people in the world.*

Travel so you can see that graduation, visit with friends far away, be part of that family wedding. Travel so that you are taking part in the lives of those important to you. It will help get you out of your own doldrums. Travel also to give yourself new perspectives; see life from a different viewpoint than that of before your loss and that of your present. A temporary change of scene to somewhere exotic can be tremendously healing. Select something that you can afford that doesn't stress your budget and GET AWAY. Immerse yourself in a new environment. Your body will relax and bless you! I was invited on a trip to Turks and Caicos with friends who play pickle-ball. My initial reaction was "NO, I don't play, and I don't feel like playing." Thankfully, I thought better of it and realized being with these others in a fun, exotic environment was exactly what I needed. I went; I didn't play pickle-ball, but I walked the beach, body surfed, sailed, kayaked, watched entertainment and took a vacation from grief to live in the present. It was tremendously healing. So were trips to horseback ride and camp with 6 fellow women, to paddle the ponds of the Adirondacks, to cruise the Erie Canal, to meet with my Book Club friends, and to visit nearby friends and relatives. A few days away in the mountains, or on the shore, or at a friends home, or in a different neighborhood or any different location can be healing.

Put your body in happy surroundings; allow your emotions to turn to the positive as you move from being immersed in grief. Expect to be on your own time frame, expect some fall-backs, but urge yourself to move forward.

Get moving physically too. It will help you to engage in whatever physical activity you like: house cleaning, redecorating, gardening, painting, walking, skiing, swimming, tennis, tai chi, yoga, etc. It really doesn't matter as long as it's something you enjoy that involves moving your body. If nothing appeals, research something new…but find it and get moving!

Identify your priorities and establish habits that support the direction you choose. Choosing your direction can be aided by various authors, mediation, counselors and life coaches, and most especially, by self-reflection and mindfulness. Journal writing and evaluation and other vehicles for mindfulness can keep you on track.

You are now well on your way to directing your present and future life . Your practices or actions are now to live beyond the sadness and distress of your past.

Go forth, enjoy the present, as the present is all we really have. Part III practices are only distantly grief-related later phase supports. How you live the rest of your life does not necessarily depend on grief. These practices are only a small sample of the input available from many sources regarding how to live optimally. It can be tremendously helpful as you use them if you are mindful and intentional of choices you are making. As you reflect upon your LIFE AFTER LOSS consider these:

## *Practices to Aid Physical and Emotional Being:*

**My thoughts and actions to honor my late beloved:**

- 

**The positives of my late relationship that incorporate into my present:**

- 

**Extensions of myself into happy surroundings and events are:**

- 

**Physical activity I employ:**

- 

**I maintain good health; I feel well and vibrant when:**

-

# *Guidepost III-B: Communicating and Relating*

It's about perspective, attitude, your choices.

"They've 'relocated,'"my sister in-law's words to describe dearly departed husbands, helped me to recognize that although Ron's body was no longer available, those loves, people, and things that he had shared with me still were. Here for me were trails, mountains, campfires, hikes, trekking poles and other gear, paddling, photography, reading, friends, relatives, grandchildren and home. And I was not ready to "relocate" yet. Although there were times when I felt like relocating off this earth, many things that I had shared with my husband were still here for me. I began to incorporate them into my new life, appreciating and letting go of Ron at the same time.

Those who evolve like I did will do well to cultivate confidants with whom to sound out ideas. Your life will present you with new opportunities, new locations, new choices. Talking with others and even with yourself, or writing letters or journals can clarify your direction. After months or years you may find yourself analyzing your past and your relationships with others, and then seeing a new or at least varied course to move away from wherever you've been in your distress. Communicate, love, forgive, accept and redesign your life!

Often, contributing to others by volunteering, baby-sitting, teaching, performing physical labor, helping a neighbor, donating clothing, furniture or money to causes that you believe in, or participating in any activity that serves someone else is a step up out of depression and toward a gratifying purposeful life connected with a community you belong to.

My sense of belonging was shaken when my spouse died. I had lost the ONE I belonged with and to. It became very important for me to communicate with those I also belonged with: my family, my close friends, my social and business groups. Their presence, hugs, commitment, care, assistance in tasks, invitations to visit and inclusion of me in important events in their lives all meant more than ever. Friends and family were open and shared their present circumstances with me. Sharing happy events such as graduations helped; sharing troubling ones such as bad diagnosis were also healing. It was extra important whenever others sought my help and presence. Hearing "Love you," getting a phone call, a text, a photo, a card, a letter, participating in a meeting and being part of a group effort were all meaningful.

You may eventually find that you would like to belong in this world as part of a couple again. You may feel that your bed is a sad, lonely place, that this is where your grief visits you most, perhaps as sadness, loneliness or even nightmares. Often people have a bed that, among other things, is a symbol of sex (thus the phrase *going to bed* means having sex) and love (thus the term *marital bed*). That may be so for you. Then it is likely that when you are fully living again you will want to love again, have sex again, *go to bed* again. Whether you do and what you allow yourself depends on your own experiences and values. Whatever that is, you may find that you or your new partner cannot incorporate the past with the present. You might find you have to redecorate the bedroom, perhaps even buy a new bed or a new house.

It has probably been a long time, maybe forever, since you've loved any other mate, or had sex with anyone other than your spouse. On the other hand, sexual love may not be an issue for you…especially initially. Grief may simply shut down desire and last for a long time. The time may come, however, when you start feeling like a sexual being again. That may or may not be connected with love.

None of the many, many books I've read about grief say anything about homes and beds. One casually mentions sex in passing…just a mention, REALLY?? You've lost your most significant other, your sexual partner, your physical and emotional link to your closest other human… and it's not even worth a mention?

What can one do about such a loss, a physical, emotional, relational and spiritual loss? Purely physically, there is the fall back position of "ringing your own chimes." Self-sex can educate you about your body, give you time to explore being a sole-soul, and ensure that you avoid getting involved physically with someone else before you are involved emotionally, intellectually, and spiritually.

Spiritually too, sex is an area in which you'll do well to know yourself as a single-again person before getting involved with someone else. You may believe that sex is the vitality of life. Now your meaningful sexual relationship is gone. Look elsewhere for your vital force. Many, religious and not, find life's force in God, especially when they have been devastated by loss. Consider also whether sexual love is something you want in your life now that your significant other has "relocated." You've perhaps never been a single adult before, certainly not one of the age you are now. Take it slowly, get confident in your own attitudes and values, think about it, discuss it with your physician, clergy, friends, and of course, your potential lover. "Be sure you're right and then go ahead! "(Davy Crockett). Read about Christian love and marriage: "Choosing to Love, Cook. 1982)

You probably will think that you'll never marry again, that you are already (still) married, or that even if you do, you really belong with your late spouse. It was the two of you who were meant for each other; this death wasn't meant to happen. I was/am comforted by the belief that love is forever, regardless of what the future may hold. You may need to conceptualize your new relationship as something different from your previous one in order to retain respect or permanence; *partner in life* may have a meaning significantly different to you from *husband* or *wife*.

You may continue veering away from any sexual relationships, approach any possible sexual relationship with great caution, reserve sex for love or marriage or indulge in a less committed sexual relationship. Widows sometimes get the reputation of being "merry" and widowers of being "players." Perhaps that's connected with their approach of enjoying casual sex, friend-sex, oh well-sex, crazy in-love too soon sex, recreational sex, or sex without love sex. The potential for loss if you allow yourself to love again can be be more threatening than that of losing a fond sexual partner. Prior experiences, personal morals and religious beliefs will all factor into your course of action.

You may want to redesign your life to include a different significant other, no significant other, a single life style, a change in house, a change in community, a change in habits. There is a wide world out there, and when you are "on your own" you may have a different perspective than when you were married or partnered with another.

Widows often move to be close to their adult children, older newly-single adults often move to adult living facilities or retirement communities. Those employed may seek variety or advancement in their jobs, or seek new jobs that allow networking with a new set of potential friends. Some enroll in school or classes to pursue an undeveloped interest.

Others decide on a more mobile life-style and spend many of their days touring in a recreational vehicle or arranging long travel experiences like hiking, trekking, or cruising. Consider what life-style changes fit the course in life that you would like to set. What you are doing now determines where you will be in the future.

Learning and teaching have always been of utmost importance in my life. Immediately following Ron's death, I had no energy for either. The first time someone suggested that I could learn from the experience of Ron's death, I was outraged! I had not yet accepted that he had passed. Emotions are temporary however, and as I gained perspective, I began to realize that I'd entered a new phase of life. I had never been a single adult responsible only for myself. I turned away from being consumed by angst to learning who I was as a single woman and to becoming a "sole-soul". Teaching and learning were still an integral part of who I was. Gradually I crafted my present to include them again. I found the book *Design the Life You Love: A Step by Step Guide to Building a Meaningful Future*, Birsel, 2015 a very good guide to synthesizing thoughts and clarifying my priorities.

After time, you may find yourself analyzing your past and relationships with others and see a new or at least varied course that will move you away from where you've been distraught. Communicate, forgive, accept, look forward and redesign your life.

A Franklin Planner, recommended by my friend Rich, was another aid to contemplating current values and priorities and setting direction in a life that had significantly changed.

## *Practices to Aid Communicating and Relating:*

**I become more other-directed by:**

- 

**I gain a sense of belonging by:**

- 

**I explore my status as a sole-soul, single adult considering sex, love, marriage, dating, and being part of a couple vs being a single person by:**

-

**I notice the following changes in routine:**

- 

**I sound-out ideas, synthesize thoughts, and clarify priorities as I design my life by :**

-

# *Guidepost III-C: Strengthening and Evolving Spiritually*

For me, carrying grief became learning how to live happily in the present while continuing to honor the past. I incorporated Ron's gifts to me in my way of life without him. I spoke or wrote of him on days during which his spirit broke the surface of the present: his birthday, our anniversary, holidays, days on which memory of him was especially vivid. I'd earlier recognized that appreciation is the key to happiness. I drew on that to be ever happy that I'd had the relationship I had had with him. There are times I still have to pull myself up short and focus on the present, the gifts that remain in my heart.

I have read that *those who focus on the past are depressed, those who focus on the future are anxious; to be happy one should focus on the present.* For years, my mantra has been "Enjoy the Present;" my answering machine announces that. I try to be mindful to live that way.

Many bereaved people become more spiritual, recognizing and celebrating God in a personal way. You can incorporate input from readings, your church, meditations or television and the internet if you are so inclined. You might cultivate your soul via nature, family, special friends, synagogue, church or mission. Whether you already have a strong spiritual foundation or cultivate one following a loss, you can benefit greatly from your faith.

Many find life-long solace contributing to charitable causes, especially causes associated with the loss of your loved one, such as Mothers Against Drunk Driving, American Heart Association or Hospice.

Some find strength spreading their newfound hope by aiding foster children, the homeless, or others in need. The love you had for your significant other may express as love for family members or members of your community. Let your spirit evolve to incorporate your present life.

## *Practices to Aid Strengthening and Evolving Spiritually:*

**Gifts and lessons I appreciate from the past that I now incorporate into my life are:**

- 

- **I maintain focus on the positives of my present by:**
- 

- **I express my appreciation and care for others by:**
-

*PRACTICE III WITH YOUR MEDITATIVE COMPANION*

*It's Nature by God; Photos by Holly Chorba,*

*Words by Various Others*

## Phase III, Life after Loss

**LIVE WELL TODAY**

## *THE CLOCK OF LIFE*

*The Clock of Life is wound but once*

*and no man has the power to tell*

*when the hands will stop,*

*at late or early hour.*

*Now is the only time you own.*

*Live, Love, Toil with a will.*

*Place no faith in time.*

*For the clock may soon be still.*

*(Carried by Al Capone )*

**NOW IS THE ONLY TIME YOU OWN**

## THE PRESENT

*You already have a*

*Gift from God.*

*It is the PRESENT.*

*Freedom from the past*

*is the present.*

*It's freedom from emotions*

*controlling your mind.*

*Ask periodically, "Am I present?"*

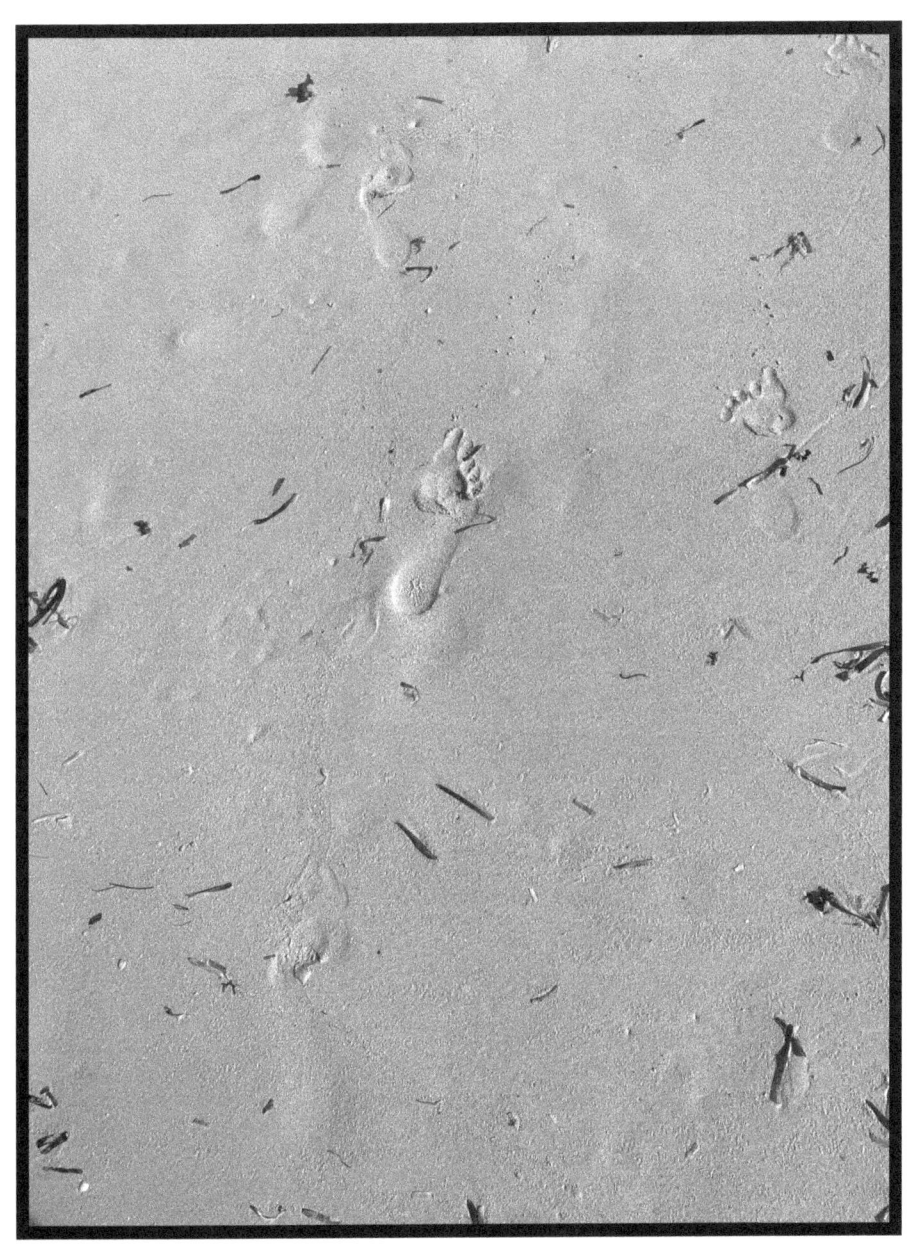

**AM I GROUNDED IN THE HERE AND NOW?**

***TODAY***

*Today is the tomorrow that you worried about yesterday.*

*When tomorrow comes today is gone.*

*"What day is it?"*

*"It's today," squeaked Piglet.*

*"My favorite day," said Pooh.*

*(A.A.Milne)*

**WHEN TOMORROW COMES TODAY IS GONE**

## *TODAY*

*Look to this day,*

*for it is the very life of life.*

*In its brief course lie all the verities and realities of your existence.*

*The Glory of Action, the Bliss of Growth, the Splendor of Beauty.*

*For yesterday is but a dream and tomorrow only a vision.*

*But today well-lived makes every yesterday a dream of happiness and every tomorrow a vision of hope.*

*Look well therefore to this day.*

*(Anonymous)*

**LOOK TO THIS DAY**

# *End Note:*

Through Phases I, II and III you have found direction and solace in the process of grieving. You are ready to focus on the many aspects of life that are NOT GRIEF. Refer back to these pages and to your journal when you'd like to review how far you've come, what has been helpful to you, or when you are considering how to help others who have lost someone they love.

*GODSPEED, and HAPPY TRAILS,*

*Holly Chorba*

# *Appendix:*

*RESOURCES (IN ORDER OF SUGGESTED USE)*

These resources were helpful to me as I traveled my own grief journey. One can find many other books, websites, movies, and television programs that can help calm your mind and steer you toward a new satisfying life. Of course, what you choose for fodder depends upon your personality and abilities. I chose these in addition to writing in journals, composing eulogies, obituaries, letters, and this book, reviewing countless photographs, creating memorial services, and sharing with others. Sharing with others was of utmost importance. I hope that you have your own people who are there for you. It is important that you know there is support and that whatever you need, you access it.

PHASE I, IMMEDIATE LOSS

## On-line Resources:

SASHA ALEX SLOAN-Until it Happens To You (Lyric Video) You Tube.SashaSloanVebo, Oct. 16, 2020

JOHANNES BRAHMS: A GERMAN REQUIEM, YouTube. DW Classical Music, Mar 31, 2021

chorbasriverflowchronicles.com/

## Books:

HOW TO HEAL A GRIEVING HEART, Virtue and Praagh, Hay House Inc., 2013.

ISBN: 978-I-4019-4337-0

DAILY WORD, A Unity Publication (Digital subscription and written publication available. unity.org or call 816-969-2069)

CHRISTMAS IN MY HEART, CHRISTMAS IN MY HANDS, unity.org , 2019. Canada BN 13252 9033RT

JESUS CALLING, Young and Nelson, HarperCollins Christian Publishing Inc., 2013. ISBN: 978 1 59145 188 4

THE MESSAGE,The Bible in Contemporary Language, Peterson, Alive Communications, Inc., 2002. ISBN: 1-57683-289-

WHAT WILL I DO WITHOUT YOU, Grindley, Kingfisher Publisher, 1999. ISBN: 978-0753451106

OPTION B, Sandberg and Grant, Knopf Publisher, 2017 ISBN: 9781524732684

BEYOND GRIEF, Staudacher, New Harbinger Pubns Inc., 1987. ISBN: 0934986436

I WASN'T READY TO SAY GOODBYE, Noel and Blair, Sourcebooks, 2008. ASIN: BOO232ZLLYY

CHOOSING TO LOVE, Cook and Cook, Gospel Light Publications, 1982. ISBN:9780830708185

PHASE II, REGAINING YOUR BALANCE

## On-line Resources:

These were particularly helpful regarding various types of memorials. All were last accessed on 7/8/2021

Cremation:  https:// en.wikipedia.org/wiki/cremation

Funeral:  https://en.wikipedia.org/wiki/funeral

Embalming:  https://www.legacy.com/advoce/the-embalming-process-how-it-works/

Viewing:  https:// en.wikipedia.org/wiki/viewiing-(funeral)

Shiva:  https://www.shiva.com/learning-center/understanding/   Smith Senior Latino Center (SLC) Copyright 2021

Celebration of Life:  https://www.loveliveson.com/100 -best-celebration-of-life-ideas-2/

Celebration of Life:  https://www.thespruce.com/what-is-a-ce;lebration-of-life-4583830

Day of the Dead (Did de los Muertos): https://artsandculture.google.com/project/dia-de-muertos    written Oct.12,2015

Coco Movie: en.wikipedia.org Coco (2017 film) edited June 28, 2021

dailyquote@abraham-hicks.com

thedailybuddha@us2.list-manage.com, 2020. All rights reserved.

## Books:

A FOREST FUNGI BATH, Chorba, Blurb, 2017. ISBN: 978-1-38-97270708

A MAN CALLED OVE, Backman, Atria Books, 2012. ISBN: 978-1-4767-3801-7

BLIND YOUR PONIES, West, Algonquin Books of Chapel Hill, 2011. ISBN: 978-1-61620-035-0

GET OUT OF YOUR OWN WAY, Goulston and Goldberg, Tarcher Perigee, 1996. ISBN: 0399519904

HOLDING ON FOR DEAR LIFE, Devivo, Liz Devivo, 2013. ISBN: 9780692755129


HOW TO GO ON LIVING WHEN SOMEONE YOU LOVE DIES by Rando, Bantam Books, 1991. ISBN: 0553352695


THE GRIEF RECOVERY HANDBOOK, James and Friedman, Harper Perennial 2009. ISBN: 9780061686078


WALKING EACH OTHER HOME: Conversations on Loving and Dying, Dass & Bush, Sounds True, 2018 .ISBN: 1683642007


WHEN YOUR SOULMATE DIES, Wolfelt, Companion Press, 2016, ISBN: 978-1-61722-242-9

# PHASE III, LIFE AFTER LOSS

## Books:

A NEW EARTH, Tolle, Penguin, 2008. ISBN: 0452289963

DESIGN THE LIFE YOU LOVE, Birsel, Ten Speed Press, 2015 ISBN :978-1-60774-881-6

LADDER OF YEARS, by Anne Tyler, Ballantine Books, 1995, ISBN: 0-449-91057-1

LEARNING TO LOVE AGAIN, by Mel Krantzler, Bantam Books, 1977, ISBN:0-553-20889-6

"PADDLING INTO THE PAST ON WELLER POND", Daniel Way; p. 24 Adirondac Michael Barrett, May-June 2020

PILLARS OF THE EARTH, Follett, Penguin Publishing Group, 1990, ISBN: 0451207149

SEX IN HUMAN LOVING, Berne M.D., Simon and Schuster, 1970, ISBN-10: 0671207717

SMART WOMEN, FOOLISH CHOICES, Cowan and Kinder, Penguin Publishing Group, 1985, ISBN: 0451158857

SOMETHING MORE, Ban Breathnach, Grand Central Publishing, 2000, ISBN-10 0446677086

MAMA GENA'S SCHOOL OF WOMANLY ARTS, Thomashauer, Simon and Schuster, 2002, ISBN:9780743226844

WHEN HUSBANDS DIE, McNally, Sunstone Press, 2005, ISBN-10: 0865344426

WOMEN ROWING NORTH, Pipher, Bloomsbury Publishing, 2019, ISBN:HB: 978-1-63286-960-9

www.ingramcontent.com/pod-product-compliance
Lightning Source LLC
Chambersburg PA
CBHW042356030426
42337CB00029B/5125